T0299585

HOW TO
MANIFEST
ANYTHING

First published in Great Britain in 2024 by Godsfield Press, an imprint of
Octopus Publishing Group Ltd
Carmelite House
50 Victoria Embankment
London EC4Y 0DZ
www.octopusbooks.co.uk

An Hachette UK Company
www.hachette.co.uk

ISBN 978-1-84181-564-0

A CIP catalogue record for this book is available from the
British Library.

Printed and bound in China
10 9 8 7 6 5 4 3 2 1

Commissioning Editor: **Louisa Johnson**
Senior Editor: **Alex Stetter**
Art Director: **Juliette Norsworthy**
Designer: **Rosamund Saunders**
Illustrator: **Agnesbic**
Copy Editor: **Caroline West**
Assistant Production Managers: **Lucy Carter and Nic Jones**

HOW TO
MANIFEST
ANYTHING

YOUR QUESTIONS ANSWERED
ON LOVE, MONEY AND MORE

VICTORIA JACKSON

GODSFIELD

CONTENTS

A NOTE FROM THE AUTHOR

Over the last decade of experimenting with, mastering and ultimately teaching the art of manifestation, I have encountered the same four words repeatedly: 'How do I manifest…?' What follows on from those words could be anything from a lottery win to a soulmate, a promotion or even a new house.

The beauty of life is that we each have our own unique desires and dreams, and manifestation – using our thoughts and the power of the Universe to create our reality – enables us to call those dreams into fruition. In my first book, *Manifesting for Beginners*, I took a deep dive into the concept of manifestation and how to weave it into the fabric of our everyday lives. But I knew that readers craved more. Something more bespoke. More personalized to their specific circumstances. And that is when the idea for *How to Manifest Anything* was born – a collection of answers to the questions I have been asked most often over the last few years.

There are many ways to teach the concept of manifestation. For some, it's about the feminine flow of releasing and receiving. For others, the focus is on the masculine energy of taking action and being decisive with your intention. For me, it's a balanced blend of both – mixing the woo-woo with the work, if you like. As a certified mindset coach specializing in Neural Energetic Wiring and Neural Energetic Encoding, an EFT (Emotional Freedom Technique) practitioner and founder of the global community, The Manifestation Collective, I offer a unique blend of spirituality, soul and science.

Over the last six years in particular, I have ticked nearly every desire off my vision board, including my debut book deal and the book you're reading right now. I've manifested my ideal house in a location I used to dream about living in, the exact car I had on my vision board a year ago, soulmate clients, beautiful friendships, hundreds of thousands of pounds into my bank account, brand collaborations, travel opportunities from LA to Hong Kong, my podcast charting at number one, being interviewed for the biggest radio station in the UK, and so much more.

How to Manifest Anything builds on all the knowledge I shared throughout *Manifesting for Beginners*, and elevates you to the next level of life. My biggest hope is that within these pages you will find the answers you have been searching for. And in turn, create a life you truly love.

Victoria
xoxo

WHAT IS MANIFESTATION?

At its very core, manifestation is the idea that we can create our reality by using the power of our thoughts. What we repeatedly choose to focus on becomes our reality.

How does this happen? By working in conjunction with the Law of Attraction – a Universal law stating that 'like attracts like'. It is said that the energy we put out into the world is the energy we attract back, just like a magnet. When we focus on the good, we see abundance in everything and magnetize abundance in every sense. When we focus on what we lack and how negative the world feels, we attract more reasons to feel unhappy. Think of manifestation as the tool we use to *consciously* choose what we attract into our lives and the Law of Attraction as the magnet that helps us attract it to us.

The Universe is a term you'll see used a lot through the pages of this book. To me, the Universe is the higher power, supporting us, helping us return to our highest self, and guiding us towards an aligned and empowered life. But for you, this could be spirit, source, angels, God – because whatever you feel most connected to will help you create the most magic.

HOW DO I MANIFEST?

Are you new to the concept of manifestation? To get you started, here are seven simple steps that offer a grounded approach to intention-setting, visualization, gratitude and building trust in the Universe.

Step 1 Begin by getting clear about what you want to manifest. This is where we set our intentions.

Step 2 Close your eyes and imagine your desire as if it is already yours. Feel the emotions associated with having it. The more vivid and emotionally connected your visualization, the stronger the signal you send to the Universe.

Step 3 Align your thoughts, beliefs and actions with your desires. For example, if you want to manifest more wealth, align your thoughts to that of a wealthy person rather than focusing on what you lack.

Step 4 Work on releasing any doubts, fears or negative beliefs that may be blocking your manifestations. Replace them with positive, empowering thoughts.

Step 5 While the Universe works its magic behind the scenes, take action steps that align with your desires.

Step 6 Maintain a gratitude journal to appreciate what you already have. When we share gratitude for what we already have in life, we open the doors to more abundance.

Step 7 Once you've put your intentions out there, release your attachment to the outcome. The 'how' and the 'when' are not our concern. Trust that the Universe is co-creating with you, but remember, it has its own timeline. Your manifestation might not happen instantly – be patient and stay in a state of gratitude and expectancy that what you desire is already yours, waiting to be delivered.

HOW TO USE THIS BOOK

Throughout the following six chapters, as we explore the idea of manifestation in life, love, friendships and family, money, career and home, you will find a collection of Q&As designed specifically to help you through different seasons of life. Perhaps you will be called to read this book in its entirety, from front to back, turning crisp corners over as a reminder to revisit something that caught your attention. Or maybe you'll dip into whichever chapter is drawing you close, answering the one question for which you've been struggling to find guidance. Whichever route you take, just know the Universe is leading you to the exact page you need.

You may notice that there is one particular topic missing from these pages – health. While I truly believe that we can use our thoughts to heal our bodies in many ways (manifestation, after all, is a mind-body connection), I am navigating so many layers and nuances myself in my own journey with an autoimmune disease that I purposely chose not to teach on this subject yet.

This personal approach is woven throughout the entire book – sharing personal experiences, client stories and powerful, tried-and-tested techniques that I have created and taught over the years. And while a technique might be highlighted for answering a particular question, everything within these pages is designed to be fluid; take what you need and apply it to your own circumstances in a way that feels aligned for you.

Most importantly, while I am here to offer guidance as a coach, I must remind you that there are no hard-and-fast rules in manifestation – my vision is for you to create a life filled with so much joy and gratitude that you become a magnet for more of what you desire. Everything else – the techniques, the exercises, the prompts – is simply a fun and actionable way of shifting your energetic state for the better.

Now let's dive in and see where the Universe leads you first…

LIFE

I'M IN AN ENERGETIC FUNK. HOW DO I SHIFT THIS?

Ah, the energetic funk. That feeling of walking through mud, with no motivation and what feels like zero connection to your vision board. Whether this energetic funk coincides with the moon, your hormonal cycle (if you experience one) or just a tough week navigating bump after bump in the road, it's natural not to feel high-vibe all of the time. Permission slip incoming – you are allowed to experience a case of 'the slumps' every now and again.

We are born with the wonderful ability to experience a range of emotions, each one designed to indicate, reflect and express something happening within our body, mind or environment. Don't be afraid to lean into your funk. It's safe to feel stuck, bored or stagnant. Sometimes, that rom-com cliché of eating ice cream straight from the tub while bingeing Netflix on the sofa really is the medicine we need.

Acknowledging the root cause of the funk can often kickstart an energetic shift on its own, especially if you are then able to take some form of action to correct your course.

As a first step, grab your journal and ask yourself these questions:

- What could this funk be indicating to me?

- Can I sense where it might stem from?

- What feels out of alignment in my life right now?

- What immediate action can I take to notice a shift in energy?

CHOOSE TO SEE THE MAGIC AROUND YOU

The following day, make a conscious decision to change how you see the world from the moment you wake up. What we project out into the world is mirrored right back to us. If we affirm the narrative that life is a constant struggle or that nothing ever works out in our favour, this is the reality we experience. The sole purpose of our reticular activating system (a system of nerves located in the brain stem) is to filter, delete or generalize the information we see, hear, smell, touch and feel, in line with our thoughts.

Whatever we choose to focus on, positive or negative, the reticular activating system will actively search for evidence to prove our thoughts to be right. For example, if you choose to focus on how bad a day you're having, every minor inconvenience, every detour and every setback will confirm that you were right: today is a tough day. But by choosing to align your vision in the direction of negativity, you miss all the amazing things happening around you.

Even if it doesn't feel like it, there truly are so many moments of magic occurring right now if you choose to see them. The door someone held for you as you struggled with your bag and coffee. A post on social media with half-price tickets to a show you wanted to see. The sun coming out after a week of grey clouds. This is where gratitude comes into play. When we're in an energetic funk, we're often in a lack mindset. But we are able to ignite a more abundant approach by focusing on the small moments of magic we can be thankful for. And the best thing about a gratitude practice? You can start at any time.

CHECK YOUR ROUTINE AND MAKE A CHANGE

For the next step, let's check in with your basic needs. Have you moved your body today? Have you filled your lungs with fresh air? Have you been outside in nature? Are you hydrated? What are you fuelling your body with? Are you getting enough sleep? Sometimes we experience an energetic funk because we've fallen out of routine with the habits that make us feel our best.

One of the simplest things we can do to shift an energetic funk is decluttering, in every sense. There's the obvious space declutter: resetting the home with a freshly made bed, watered plants and wiped-down surfaces. But then there's also the digital declutter: muting people who don't make us feel our best selves online, deleting old photos and screenshots on our phone, and uninstalling unused apps. Remove yourself from tech altogether if you can. Have a digital detox. Scrolling does nothing for your energy except deplete it.

And finally, a powerful shift to reset your energy and move out of a slump is to make a change. Any change. A change in the way the furniture in your living room is arranged. A change of morning routine. A change in the podcasts you listen to. A change in your working environment. A change in your walking route. A change of hair colour.

Change disrupts the monotony that can cause us to experience a lower mood. This disruption could be as simple as swapping to your less dominant hand when brushing your teeth, but it can also serve as a catalyst for rediscovering our goals and purpose. Are you still as connected to your goals as you were six months ago? Do you need to re-evaluate your vision?

IF YOUR GOAL CHANGES

Goal setting shouldn't be linear. It shouldn't come with a fear of changing your mind. The beauty of life lies in its fluidity. In the ebbs and flows of what we crave and what we no longer feel called towards. If you have a goals list or a vision board, check in and see how aligned you feel with this. There's nothing like setting a new vision for this next chapter in your life to clear out stagnant energetic blocks.

I DON'T KNOW WHAT TO MANIFEST. WHAT SHOULD I DO?

There will be points during your manifestation journey, especially in the very beginning, where you're not quite sure what it is you want to call into your life. If you've always felt as if life just happens, then the realization that we are in full control of the ship can feel a little overwhelming. If, right now, you're struggling to know what your dream life looks like, here are five things to consider.

WHAT WOULD BRING YOU JOY?
One of the most important factors in the manifestation process is focusing on joy. As mentioned on page 17, when we feel in a more positive frame of mind, we vibrate at a higher frequency and therefore become magnetic to things that will keep us in this elevated state.

Take a moment to journal and ask yourself, 'What would feel good to manifest right now?' The key here is to think about what you really want and ignore the 'shoulds', the opinions of others, or whatever the latest social media trend dictates.

Alignment doesn't come from trying to fit into a mould that isn't the perfect shape for you.

WHAT DO YOU NOT WANT?

Sometimes we can discover what we truly want in life by taking a look at what we don't want. Are there things in your life that you'd like to change? For example, maybe you're tired of a long commute to work and you'd like to manifest a job closer to home. Or perhaps you're tired of feeling financially anxious every month and you'd like to manifest more income through a passion project. Gaining clarity on what you don't want in life can help you figure out what it is you want to magnetize to you.

WHAT DOES YOUR IDEAL DAY LOOK LIKE?

Another way to gain clarity is to journal about your ideal day. Find a quiet spot and allow yourself to relax before taking pen to paper. Write a diary entry as if you've just had your ideal day and describe in detail what happened, from the moment you woke up to what was in your wardrobe, from how you spent the afternoon to completing your evening skincare routine. Include everything that matters to you, no matter how small or seemingly insignificant. There's no such thing as a small wish to the Universe.

WHAT WOULD MAKE YOU HAPPIER IN THIS VERY MOMENT?

Instead of focusing on the future, think about how you feel right now. When you're in a positive, high-vibrational energy, manifestations can appear quickly. What small things that bring joy can you start working on attracting? Perhaps a phone call from someone you've lost touch with? Some money for a spa day?

WHERE ARE YOU OUT OF ALIGNMENT?

When you're unsure about what to manifest, it can be helpful to look at the areas of your life that feel out of alignment. Which parts of your daily routine feel out of sync? Are you looking to manifest a better morning routine? Does your home environment feel out of alignment? Perhaps you no longer feel connected to the work you do. Look at what needs a shift in energy and start planning your manifestations from there.

IT'S OKAY TO PAUSE

Remember, these are your intentions, your manifestations, and your visions for your future. It's okay to try something, change your mind and then go in a new direction. If you're struggling to know what to manifest, take a break and reset. Treat this time as a way of grounding yourself and understanding your desires. Journalling and meditation are great ways to do this. Give yourself permission to sit in the energy you're in now and allow the Universe to deliver clarity and direction when the time is right.

MY MANIFESTATION HASN'T ARRIVED YET. WHAT AM I DOING WRONG?

First, let's begin by affirming the following: there is no such thing as 'wrong' in manifestation. However, you might want to consider some shifts and changes in order to realign yourself with your desired outcome.

When we begin to manifest, we can become stuck on the 'how' and the 'when'. And if our desires don't appear in the timeframe we set in our minds, it can leave us feeling deflated and confused. It's like we've been ghosted by the Universe.

HOW TO CHANGE YOUR MINDSET

A simple way to shift your focus is to list all the reasons why it *is* possible for you to have your particular desire. Why you *are* worthy of receiving it. Where focus goes, energy flows. Plus, whether we ask the subconscious a negative or positive question, it will still go in search of evidence to support what we are asking. Why not ask it a positive-led question, and see the positive solutions that come to light?

Sometimes we hear stories of people magnetizing thousands of dollars into their bank account overnight or soulmates bumping into each other in the street. But let's be honest, these are anomalies. Yes, everything you envision is available for you, but the Universe may need to work behind the scenes before your desire can be delivered. Here are three questions to ask yourself when there is a delay in your manifestation arriving.

DO I BELIEVE IT TO BE POSSIBLE FOR ME?

One of the biggest pockets of resistance in the concept of 'Ask, Believe, Receive' is believing it's possible to have what you desire. Check in on your self-worth. Do you feel worthy of having your vision-board life? If you're facing resistance to this question, why *don't* you feel worthy? Listen closely to the voice in your head – does it resemble anyone in your family or friendship group? Subconsciously you may have taken on others' beliefs of what is possible for you, rather than your own.

AM I TRYING TO CONTROL THE OUTCOME?

If you struggle with the need to control, the concept of manifestation – where we are being asked to let go of the 'how' and 'when' and trust in divine timing – can feel challenging at times. Control is a protection mechanism. The more we can control our surroundings, the less likely we are to activate our fight-or-flight mode.

One affirmation to repeat if you struggle with trying to control the outcome is: 'It is this or something better', knowing that when you release the tight grip you have around your manifestation, it will either be what you desire or something *even better* than you could have imagined.

If the 'how' and 'when' is something you just can't let go of, then why not open your mind to all the amazing ways in which your desires could be delivered? You can do this by making a list of every weird, wild and mundane way your manifestation might come to fruition.

HAVE I TAKEN ACTION TO MEET THE UNIVERSE HALFWAY?

The last question to ask yourself is: have I put the action into the Law of Attraction and met the Universe halfway? While some manifestations can appear with little or no action, taking some form of aligned step forward can help turn your vision board into reality in a much quicker timeframe. What does aligned action mean? Aligned action is moving forward in a way that feels good in your soul. It feels exciting. It feels right in your gut. For example, maybe you're manifesting a new job and suddenly you think of reaching out to a former colleague. Aligned action could be sending them an email to say you're looking for new opportunities.

WHAT ARE SOME DAILY MANIFESTING RITUALS I CAN DO?

There are a wealth of experts in the field of manifestation and personal development who talk about the power of a morning routine, and in many ways I agree with the idea of setting an intention for the day ahead and consciously choosing our energetic state of being.

However, from experience, having a strict morning routine doesn't always align with each of our unique energy flows – what works for one person might not work for the next. Enter the spiritual self-care pick and mix, a tool belt of techniques, if you like, that you can dip into throughout the day.

MORNING MIRROR MEETING

Each morning while you are getting ready, look into the mirror and list the following:

Three things you love about yourself today – including your energy, the physical qualities you choose to appreciate that day, and the characteristics that make you uniquely you.

Three things you are grateful for from yesterday – big or small, reaffirm to the Universe all that you are thankful for, so you can welcome more of the same.

Three affirmations to guide your day – the key to affirmations strengthening new neural pathways and weakening old, negative beliefs is to use language that resonates with you. For example, if you struggle with body image, then repeating the affirmation 'I love my body' might not be as powerful as something like 'I am thankful that my body allowed me to wake up this morning', simply because the latter may resonate with you more.

SHOWER VISUALIZATION

Shower visualizations are incredibly powerful, as you can not only spend time connecting with your future self, but also lean into the metaphor of using water to wash away anything you no longer want to carry with you.

As you shower, visualize how you'll feel when your desires come to fruition. Allow that energy to sit with you for a moment as you create a movie in your mind. And as the shower comes to an end, think about a belief, a habit, or anything that is stopping this dream from coming to fruition, and imagine the water washing it down the plughole.

JOURNALLING

If you are being called to make journalling a part of your manifestation routine, there is real power in returning to the same prompts each day for clarity, focus and alignment. Try these:

- What do I *get* to do today, rather than have to do?
- What is my biggest priority today and how can I make sure this is taken care of?
- What belief isn't serving me today?
- What one action could I take today towards achieving my vision-board self?
- What will bring me the most joy today and how can I implement this?

ACTIVELY EXPAND YOUR MIND

Expand your mind to what is possible for you by actively seeking people who have what you desire. Allow your subconscious to see what is possible and instead of falling into the trap of comparison, explore what model that person has used to attract what they want.

For example, if you wish to build your own business, you can search for people on social media who are currently in full-time employment but also building a passion project on the side. Can you see what habits they have? Can you see from what they share how they manage their time? This isn't necessarily about emulating someone else's blueprint, but more about seeing how they take action and understanding what is possible for you.

REGULAR CHECK-INS

There will be moments throughout the day when you can check in on your energy, mindset and physiology, perhaps while making coffee, brushing your teeth, eating lunch or even when travelling (whatever mode of transport you take). Use these moments to note whether you're in an abundant or lack mindset and realign your physiology accordingly. Our physiology – our body language, the way we stand, the way we move, and so on – can have an instrumental effect on our behaviour and actions. This is why the Power Pose, a somatic technique where you stand feet apart with your hands on your hips, has been shown to increase feelings of confidence and assertiveness.

WHAT SHOULD I DO IF I NO LONGER WANT WHAT I'VE MANIFESTED?

This question is actually more common than you might think. I'm often asked, 'I've manifested something and it isn't quite what I expected. What do I do now?' And woven throughout that question can be an element of guilt. After all, aren't we supposed to be grateful for what the Universe delivers? There are a number of ways we can positively reframe this because, on my watch, guilt isn't something we should have to navigate when it comes to manifestation.

Receiving your manifestation and then realizing it isn't what you expected provides the perfect chance to go back and refine your cosmic shopping list. A cosmic shopping list is a list of specifics. How you want your manifestation to make you feel, what you want it to look like, feel like, be like. For example, if you were manifesting a new house, your cosmic shopping list might say what neighbourhood it is in, how many bedrooms you'd like, what style of house it is, if there is a garden, or even a gym and a cinema room (remember there is no limit to what the Universe can help you manifest).

While we dive deeper into the subject of dream homes on pages 136–9, let's take a look here at the idea of manifesting your soulmate. The Universe delivered someone that ticked most boxes on your cosmic shopping list, but there just wasn't a spark, no matter how hard you tried to ignite it. Plus, they didn't communicate well and you realized as time went on that clear communication is a non-negotiable for you. Experiences, people, opportunities, and so on, are sent into our lives for us to fully understand what it is we desire. It's impossible for us to know if something is right for us until we've experienced it. Afterall, we don't know what we don't know.

Manifesting a new job is another example of thinking we desire something, and then the reality of the manifestation being different. A member of my community shared a story with me about how she thought her dream job had materialized, but three months down the line she realized that working alone at home wasn't what she actually wanted. Yet she struggled with the guilt of manifesting this role and feeling ungrateful. But my advice was this. How about we see this as a moment to refine our specifics and to release this role for someone who truly desires it. That way, there is no guilt attached because even though the Universe delivered what we thought we wanted, by releasing it we're allowing someone else to receive their manifestation, and we clear any blockages around us receiving what it is we truly want. In this instance, a job within a team working in an uplifting, lively environment.

How beautiful is the reframe that allows us to be grateful for what the Universe delivers, but feel safe in the knowledge that if we press return to sender (as we would in real life if something wasn't right for us), the same manifestation can make its way to someone else. We don't ever throw a desire away; we pass the baton to someone else to tick off their vision board.

So it's okay to say no. Listen to your gut instinct. Your internal compass will never guide you off track. Think of it as refining the algorithm of the Universe. The more we refine and say no to things, the more we'll recognize what is truly right for us. It is safe to say thank you, then to release our manifestation back into the world for someone else and to refine our vision once more.

MANIFESTATION MYTH BUSTING

Myth: One negative thought can halt my manifestations.

Truth: Rather than a single negative thought having the power to disrupt your manifestation, turn your focus to the overall consistent pattern of your thoughts and emotions, your beliefs, and your ability to maintain a positive and aligned mindset over time.

Q

IF 'LIKE ATTRACTS LIKE', AM I GOING TO MANIFEST NEGATIVE THINGS INTO MY LIFE WHEN IN THE DEPTHS OF A CHALLENGING TIME, SUCH AS FEELING GRIEF?

In the toxic depths of the internet, it is said that when bad things happen, it is because we have manifested them. I disagree. The Universal Law of Rhythm, sister to the Law of Attraction, states that there are natural ebbs and flows in life. Just as seasons come and go, like when the snow melts to make way for the sprouts of spring flowers to break through the soil, so will challenging moments. Back and forth. Light and dark. Life and death are part of being cyclical beings.

One bad thought doesn't instantly manifest. If that was the case, the world would be a very challenging place to live. And while there is certainly truth to the compound effect – the more we focus on the negative around us, the tougher our lives can feel – this is a reminder that you have not manifested all the negative things in your life as some form of punishment for not being a ball of sunshine every second of every day.

Of course, it's important to acknowledge the power of thoughts and attitudes in shaping our reality, but it is also crucial to understand that grief and challenging times are natural and valid human experiences. Sometimes life is just hard. Really hard. And sometimes we can't control what is happening around us, especially other people's behaviour and actions. But we can control how we react and how we take responsibility for our emotions, behaviour and actions.

For a moment, let us consider the Abraham Hicks emotional guidance scale, which is designed to help you move through a range of emotions – from the lower end of the scale where fear, grief and despair sit, through to the higher end of the scale where you'll find enthusiasm, happiness and passion – by moving up the scale in incremental steps.

If you are vibrating at a lower frequency, experiencing grief, it is near impossible to shoot to the top of the scale to feel joy and eagerness. Instead, can you move up the scale to feel boredom? And then hopefulness. And then up the scale again to focus on gratitude. And then a glimmer of optimism?

Experiencing grief is a normal response to loss, regardless of what that loss may be, and it is essential to give yourself permission to go through the grieving process. It's important to allow yourself to heal and gradually open up to more positive experiences when you're ready.

When that time comes, this book has been designed so you can turn to it as your Manifestation Guide 101 – the beginning of this chapter on moving out of energy funks being the perfect place to start, before you begin building a life that fills your cup again.

Q

HOW DO I TAKE MY MANIFESTING TO THE NEXT LEVEL?

If there was one element of manifesting I could teach over and over, it would be embodiment. Embodiment is incredibly empowering. With regards to manifestation, it is the art of fully inhabiting your future self within the present moment and aligning your thoughts, feelings and actions with the version of you that already has everything you desire. The version of us that we visualize is already available to us. Despite being in a different reality to what we desire, we have the ability to shift into a new way of thinking and acting. We have the ability to choose a different state of mind. To change our self-identity. Our self-image. To make different choices. To consciously alter our model of the world.

By consciously aligning your thoughts, emotions and actions to that of your future self you become a magnetic force for your manifestations. The Universe responds to what you think, mirroring back exactly what you believe and feel to be true about yourself. What is your reflection saying? Here are five ways you can move into your future self today:

YOUR FUTURE WARDROBE

They say dress for the job you want, but how about dressing for the life you want? How does the vision-board version of you dress? What clothes make them feel confident? What scent do they wear? What hairstyle do they have?

How you choose to dress can have an incredible effect on your energy and mindset throughout the day. Think about how you feel when you're in your comfies compared to when you put on your favourite outfit. Begin by pulling together outfit ideas on Pinterest and create a style vision board. While you might want to rush to buy new pieces that align to your future self, I suspect there are already a whole host of options within your current wardrobe that you can restyle and rework.

DECISION-MAKING

Embodiment isn't just about your appearance, though; your future self is also defined by the choices they make and the actions they take. Begin aligning your daily decisions with those of your future self. Ask yourself, 'What would they do in this situation?' By making choices that are aligned with your desired outcome, you establish a sense of harmony between your current reality and the life you are manifesting.

CULTIVATING HABITS FOR SUCCESS

Habits play a significant role in shaping our lives. If you want to embody your future self, it is crucial to cultivate habits that support your desired reality. Identify the habits your ideal self possesses and start integrating them into your daily routine. Whether it is waking up early to journal, practising gratitude or dedicating time to personal development, each habit will bring you one step closer to becoming the person who has everything they desire.

EMBRACE RADICAL AUTHENTICITY

Embodying your future self requires you to embrace your authentic self. Release the need to conform to societal expectations and honour your true self unapologetically. Speak your truth, express your passions and surround yourself with people who uplift and support your journey. Where are you not living authentically right now? Use this as a journal prompt and see what bubbles to the surface.

STEP INTO FEARLESSNESS

Your future self is fearless in pursuing their dreams and goals because they know life is too short to be mediocre. Identify one fear or limiting belief that has been holding you back and take a bold step to conquer it. Whether it is speaking in a meeting, signing up for a course to expand your knowledge and skills, or starting a passion project, face your fears head on and celebrate yourself each step of the way.

LOVE

HOW DO I MANIFEST MY SOULMATE?

Do you believe in soulmates? I do. I believe there are people in this world who are perfectly aligned to the vision of what we desire. I do not, however, think that there is just one soulmate in the world for each person. I believe we can discover soulmate love in friendships, in different seasons of life, and in different people. And I believe that we have the power to manifest soulmate love into our lives.

WHAT ARE YOU LOOKING FOR?
Manifesting soulmate love in a romantic sense begins with understanding what you desire from your partner. Throughout this book, I speak of specificity and how nailing down the details of your manifestation can help the Universe understand what to deliver. However, while it is certainly powerful to create a cosmic shopping list of the characteristics and personality traits you desire in your partner, being too specific about their physical traits could throw the Universe off track. For example, if you become so fixated on attracting someone tall, dark and handsome, you might just miss the average-height, blonde and adorable soulmate being sent in your direction.

Your cosmic shopping list could include traits such as having an amazing sense of humour and a love of adventure, being a great cook or strong communicator, or being family-orientated, kind-hearted, loyal, spontaneous, ambitious or playful – can you see how none of these are dependent on someone's hair colour or height?

Once you are clear on the kind of person you are manifesting, be intentional with dating. Let the Universe know you are serious by not continuing to waste time and energy on people with glaringly obvious red flags. We are not in the business of accepting less than we desire, despite what someone else may have led you to believe over the years.

Ironically, sometimes the Universe will send a frog or two, to help you understand what it is you truly desire – and, more importantly, what you don't want in a partnership. Listen to your gut. Your inner guidance will never lead you astray and this includes when manifesting love. If something is telling you this isn't your person, release them with gratitude for the clarity they provided and move on.

One of the biggest stumbling blocks I see people experience is the limiting belief that there isn't a person out there who embodies everything they desire. But if you embody everything you desire, then why can't someone else? If you are a multifaceted human, with varying interests and views on the world, then why can't someone else be? You are living proof that it is possible.

BE THE LOVE YOU WANT TO ATTRACT

It is so important to embody your cosmic shopping list. You attract what you are. So for example, if you desire someone who loves adventure, yet you rarely leave the house, it's near impossible for your energies to align. Or if you want to manifest a dream partner who is a great communicator, but you struggle to say what is on your mind in other areas of your life, you are not an energetic match with what you are calling in. Rehearse for success and live as if your soulmate is in your reality. Send good morning texts to yourself to read when you wake up. Make space for them at home. Clear out your bedside table. Add an extra toothbrush to the bathroom. Buy the underwear that makes you feel amazing now, rather than waiting. Experiment with new recipes. Spray a scent such as aftershave or perfume that evokes the emotions of your future partner.

CELEBRATE ROMANTIC LOVE

If it feels like you have been trying to manifest your soulmate for eternity, it is natural to experience resistance when you are exposed to people in love. It could be strangers kissing or a film with a fairytale ending. But instead of becoming cynical about love, how can you celebrate it? How can you appreciate it and show the Universe that you really do love, love.

On the subject of fairytale endings, consider what content you are regularly absorbing. For example, if you are consistently listening to songs about heartbreak, or watching films where someone is unfaithful, you are programming your mind to expect much of the same. Instead, romanticize your life. Enjoy small moments of magic, such as lighting a candle or curling up with a good book. Date yourself – venture out on a solo date to a coffee shop or take yourself to the cinema. Be present in the now and soak up the joy that comes with learning who you are and discovering what you like. You can only truly welcome love into your life when you no longer feel like you're waiting for the other half of you. You are whole already.

TRUST THE UNIVERSE

Finally, trust in divine timing. As frustrating as it can feel when someone says, 'They'll appear when you least expect them to', manifesting your soulmate comes down to being in the energy of joy and contentment as much as possible and making your life feel so fulfilled that you regard anything extra that comes into it as a bonus. A romantic, loyal, spontaneous, passionate bonus that can cook and makes you laugh until your stomach aches.

SOULMATE CEREMONY

Step 1 Find somewhere comfortable to sit, then light a candle. In your journal, write a love letter to your soulmate in the present tense, as if they have already manifested. Share how they make you feel, talk about how incredible it feels for them to be walking through life alongside you, and describe how you spend your time together – be as vulnerable and open as possible.

Step 2 Close your eyes, take three deep breaths, inhaling through your nose and exhaling through your mouth, allowing yourself to relax. Visualize life with your soulmate. Focus on how you feel, knowing the relationship you dreamed about has become your reality. As this energy of love and excitement begins to expand throughout your body, imagine yourself becoming a magnet for your manifestation, knowing that at this moment the Universe is aligning the dots so your paths ultimately cross.

Step 3 Place a crystal such as rose quartz or rhodonite (known for their healing properties) under your pillow. Release your desire, knowing that the Universe is now conspiring how and when to bring your soulmate into your reality.

I THOUGHT I HAD MANIFESTED THE PERFECT PARTNER, BUT IT DIDN'T WORK OUT. WHAT HAPPENED?

Heartbreak is a challenging season to navigate, especially when you were certain the Universe had delivered your soulmate. But things began to unravel and doubts crept in that made you question if you were meant for each other after all.

The Universe will always connect us to people for a reason. There is no such thing as a chance meeting. No coincidence of stumbling across someone. Whether it be to teach us a lesson or guide us to count a blessing, there is a reason why this person came into your life. Perhaps the timing of the relationship wasn't as aligned as it could have been. As the saying goes, what is meant for you will never pass you by. If this truly is your soulmate, there's no doubt about it: they will return when you are both energetically aligned to support, love and be with one another.

The most important question we can ask is, what did you learn from this relationship? Let's look at your cosmic shopping list – did this person truly embody everything you desire? Remove the rose-tinted

JOURNAL EXERCISES TO HEAL HEARTBREAK

- What are the dominant emotions you are experiencing right now, and how do they appear in your daily life?

- Explore any recurring patterns or behaviours in your past relationships. Do any common themes emerge? What have you learned from these patterns?

- List five qualities or traits that make you unique and valuable as an individual.

- Consider writing a Letter of Resolution to your ex-partner (even if you don't intend to send it), expressing your feelings, thoughts and any unresolved matters. This can help you find a sense of closure. For more on writing a Letter of Resolution, see page 131.

- Describe the kind of relationship you envision for your future. What qualities and values are important to you in a partner and what boundaries will you establish?

- Journal on the self-care activities that bring you comfort and peace. How can you include more of these practices into your daily routine to support your healing process?

- Examine any feelings of anger or resentment towards your ex-partner. How can you work on forgiving them and releasing these negative emotions for your own well-being?

- Write down three things you are grateful for each day. This can help shift your focus towards positive aspects of your life.

- Describe a goal or passion you'd like to pursue now that you have more time and energy. How can you take steps towards achieving this goal?

- Write a letter to yourself as if you were offering advice and comfort to a close friend going through the same situation.

- Document your progress over time. Compare your initial entries to your current thoughts and emotions.

glasses for just a moment and ask yourself: did you settle for less than you deserve because this person embodied *some* of the things you desire in a soulmate? Did your values align; were your visions for the future woven in the same thread? While the initial heartbreak can feel like your lungs are struggling for air, once you have had space to breathe, begin to consider how the Universe might just have removed something from your life to make way for something better. Heartbreak is, unfortunately, part of the tapestry of manifesting soulmate love. Every challenge you face, every person you meet who isn't quite right, and every frog you kiss is shaping you and your desires.

The key now is not to get so deep into the mentality of 'why me' that you create resistance to someone new entering your life. Grieve for the potential that is no more, and then ask yourself how you can move back into the energy of love. This was just a warm-up act. The Universe is preparing a love so perfectly suited for you that you'll understand in hindsight why everything up until now has led you to this point. Mark my words.

HOW DO I MANIFEST MY EX BACK?

If you are dipping into this chapter, skimming the words until you find the magic spell to manifest your ex-partner back, then I'm afraid you might be disappointed (initially). I have received hundreds of messages from people over the years asking this very question, each one filled with heartbreak and the hope that manifestation will help magnetize their love back to them. Manifestation could definitely do that. Ask the Universe, believe it to be possible, and be open to receiving: the concept is the same regardless of what you want to attract into your life.

However, I want you to take what I write next with the love with which it is intended. The Universe removed this person from your life for a reason. That reason might not be clear right now. In fact, it could feel overwhelmingly confusing. But by spiritually manipulating someone else's life path by manifesting them back into your life, your time with them is, unfortunately, limited. If someone is not meant to be a permanent fixture in your life, the Universe will find a way, time and time again, to remove them. No matter how hard you visualize or journal on being reunited.

How about we focus on calling the energy of love into our lives instead? Rather than honing in on a specific person, focus rather on filling our days with as much joy and gratitude as possible. And if that person returns, without force, we know it was meant to be. Imagine how amazing it would feel to know that your partner came back into your life with free will, rather than being manipulated with manifestation? That you didn't have to force a 'coincidental' meeting down the supermarket aisle, but instead the Universe led you to bump into them organically. That you were on their mind so much that they couldn't help but message to ask how you are, without you having to journal on attracting them back every single night.

THAT PERSON MAY BE A LESSON

One thing to note is this: the Universe could very well bring someone back into your life so you can cut energetic cords and tie up loose ends once and for all. They may return for you to realize that it isn't the relationship you deserve after all. As much as this question can feel like a dagger to the heart, ask yourself: what is pulling you to manifest someone who no longer wanted to be with you? Toxic relationships can be painful but addictive at the same time. Despite the unbearable lows, the highs feel indescribable. Some people are more comfortable with a negative familiarity than they are with an unfamiliar yet positive possibility. We find comfort in the familiar, even if we know it doesn't serve us. Which parts of the relationship didn't serve you? Made you feel 'less than'? Made you question yourself? Now is the time to understand why the Universe sent this person into your life and, more importantly, why it removed them.

Remember, the Universe will take out the trash so you don't have to. Trust in the divine timing of your life and, for now, focus on healing.

HOW DO I GET MY CYNICAL PARTNER ON BOARD WITH MANIFESTING?

I know first hand how exciting it feels to discover the concept of manifestation and being eager to share this magic with everyone you know. We understand just how powerful manifesting is and how it can change lives. But, as with anything out of the norm, the idea that we can create our reality with our thoughts can be met with scepticism and resistance. Especially from those closest to us.

OPEN COMMUNICATION

The first step in introducing manifestation to your partner is to have an open and honest conversation. Share your beliefs and experiences with each other without judgement, dismissal or interruption. Create a safe space for them to express their doubts and concerns. Remember, it is essential to respect their perspective, even if it differs from yours. Open communication is the foundation for bridging the gap between scepticism and belief.

SHARE PERSONAL EXPERIENCES

Personal experiences can be a powerful way to illustrate the effectiveness of manifestation. Share your own success stories and how manifestation has positively impacted your life. Hearing about tangible results can make the concept more relatable for your partner. Sharing your journey can help them see the potential benefits of embracing this practice, especially as a level of trust has already been developed.

PROVIDE CREDIBLE RESOURCES

If your partner is resistant to spirituality and more inclined toward the science behind manifestation, offer them credible resources that blend the two worlds. Point them towards books, articles or documentaries that discuss the psychology and scientific principles behind manifestation. The likes of Dr Tara Swart and Dr Joe Dispenza combine neuroscience with manifestation, sharing scientific evidence of manifestation working, away from the woo-woo.

START SMALL WITH MINI EXPERIMENTS

Instead of diving headfirst into grand manifestations, start small to build trust and belief. Encourage your partner to be curious and open-minded by conducting simple manifestations together – manifesting a parking spot or a free coffee can be a light-hearted way to introduce the concept without overwhelming them. Let them see first-hand how their thoughts can influence their reality in seemingly small ways.

LEAD BY EXAMPLE

One of the most effective ways to inspire your partner is to lead by example. Embrace manifestation in your own life and demonstrate its positive impact. Show them how you set intentions, maintain a positive mindset, and work towards your goals. When they witness your personal growth and success, they may become more inclined to explore manifestation themselves.

SEEK COMPROMISE AND RESPECT BOUNDARIES

Respect is crucial when introducing new beliefs or practices into a relationship. If your partner remains sceptical, seek compromise and respect their boundaries. Manifestation should never be forced upon someone. Allow them to choose their level of involvement or interest in the practice. It is essential to maintain a healthy balance between pursuing your interests and nurturing your relationship.

Getting your sceptical partner on board with manifestation requires patience, empathy and effective communication. Remember that everyone's journey towards acceptance and understanding is unique, and the key is to foster a loving and compassionate relationship throughout the process. With time and persistence, your partner may come to appreciate the power of manifestation and its potential to transform their life.

SOME MINI MANIFESTATION IDEAS

- Flowers
- A call or text from someone
- Green traffic light
- A small amount of money
- A compliment
- Finding something you've lost

IS IT POSSIBLE TO MANIFEST MORE SELF-LOVE AND CONFIDENCE?

Absolutely. The first step on this deeply personal journey of self-love and confidence is identifying what is plaguing you with doubt in the first place. Where are you the most cynical? Is it around your appearance, your abilities or something else entirely? Be honest with yourself about your insecurities, as this is the starting point for growth.

YOUR INNER FRIEND

At this stage in the journey, it's time to lean on your inner friend. Imagine your best friend is sitting with you, listening while you list all of the reasons why you don't think you are worthy enough. What would they say to counter these self-doubts and critical thoughts? Let your inner friend talk. A little compassion can go a long way when manifesting something as powerful as self-love.

YOUR SELF-TALK

Language plays a key role in how successful we are at manifesting. What we say about ourselves is what we notice in the world around us. As mentioned previously on page 17, the Universe will hold a mirror up and reflect back the energy you put out into the world – and that means the way you speak about yourself. Be conscious of catching negative self-talk and replace it with positive affirmations and reframes. Consistently challenge your inner critic with words of love, and after a while notice how your thought patterns begin to shift as you create new positive pathways in the subconscious mind.

NOTICE OTHERS

Another way that your manifestation can be reflected back to you is seeing others radiate the energy you desire. Instead of feeling envious and asking why that isn't your reality, celebrate other people for all they are. Recognizing someone else's self-love and confidence doesn't diminish your own. The Universe is simply showing you what is possible.

TAKE SMALL STEPS

Now, take a moment to imagine the most confident version of yourself. How does that version of you show up in life? What actions do they take? Take small but intentional steps in implementing these actions into your daily life and, over time, those layers of self-doubt will begin to show cracks until they weaken completely.

YOUR FRIENDSHIPS

One of the most important things you can do when manifesting more self-love and confidence is to surround yourself with people on the frequency you want to match. People who build you up and believe in your potential. Negative opinions from other people – be it family, friends or a previous relationship (can you hear a certain person's voice as you read this?) – can hinder your self-love journey, so embrace friendships that support and encourage your growth.

RIPPLE EFFECT

We know that the energy we put out into the world is the energy we receive back, which is why giving sincere compliments to others opens our energetic field to receive them as well, creating a beautiful cycle that boosts our self-esteem and creates a ripple effect of positivity all around us.

SHOW GRATITUDE

Part of the manifestation process is to focus on gratitude for what we already have and to celebrate what is currently in our reality, so with that said, what can you acknowledge and be thankful for right now? On page 27 I share a powerful technique called Morning Mirror Meeting, which is an incredible way to align to the energy of self-love and confidence as you get ready to start the day.

PRACTISE SELF-CARE

Finally, remember that you are worthy of self-care (for more on this, see page 152). Enjoy those small moments of self-indulgence, whether it's a long, relaxing, candlelit bath, a book and a cup of tea, a peaceful walk in nature, or nourishing your body with wholesome food. These acts of self-care replenish your energy and contribute to your self-love journey, highlighting to the Universe what you would like to receive more of.

SOME SELF-LOVE AFFIRMATIONS

- I embrace my imperfections as unique qualities that make me who I am.
- My self-worth is not determined by the opinions of others.
- I am enough, just as I am, and I don't need to prove myself to anyone.
- I deserve love, happiness and all the good things life has to offer.
- I forgive myself for past mistakes and choose to learn and grow from them.
- I love and accept myself unconditionally, flaws and all.
- I let go of comparison and focus on my own journey.
- My self-love grows stronger every day.
- I deserve all the love and kindness that I give to others.
- I am open to receiving compliments and believe them when I hear them.
- I am a work-in-progress, and that's okay. I love and accept myself at every stage of my journey.

HOW CAN I MANIFEST BETTER SEX?

Manifestation can have a powerful impact on our sex life. When applied with a blend of curiosity, self-discovery and open communication, this more holistic approach has the potential not only to enhance your sexual experiences but also to deepen the connection you share with your partner.

SELF-DISCOVERY

The journey towards manifesting better sex begins with self-discovery. It's a process that invites you to explore your innermost desires and preferences. Take the time to truly understand what you want, both physically and emotionally. This first step is not only about defining your desires, but also about ensuring that they align with your partner's needs. When you are in harmony with yourself and your partner, better sex can naturally unfold.

Self-discovery is also about understanding your values, boundaries and emotional needs. When you have a clear understanding of these, you can better navigate your intimate experiences and communicate effectively with your partner.

REFLECT ON PAST EXPERIENCES

Another essential aspect of manifesting better sex is reflecting on positive past experiences. If possible, think back to moments that brought you pleasure, those instances that left you feeling satisfied, and the magnetic energy of desire that you've experienced before, even if it was with a different partner or even while spending time exploring your own body. By revisiting these memories and reconnecting to the emotions they evoke, you can access the sensuality and desire that is already stored within you, helping you become a magnet for it, so it becomes part of your current reality once more.

MANIFEST THROUGH JOURNALLING

While sitting in bed with a notebook and pen might seem like the opposite of what you'd think will manifest more action between the sheets, attracting a better sex life often starts with a change in mindset. One way to achieve this is through journalling. Journalling allows you to put your desires into words and envision them as if they were already your reality.

Describe the sensations, emotions and connection you crave from your intimate moments. This practice not only helps you clarify your desires but also sends a potent message to your subconscious mind, aligning it with your sexual goals. As you write about your ideal sexual experiences, you are not only setting intentions but also actively participating in the process of attracting those desires into your life.

EMBODY YOUR DESIRES

Embodying your desires involves a mind-body practice in which you cultivate a deep sense of self-desirability. Engage in activities that make you feel sexy and confident, whether it's through regular exercise, meditation or self-care routines, for example. When you feel desirable and confident in your own skin, you naturally radiate that energy, which makes you more magnetic to your partner. This embodiment of your desires is about enhancing not only your physical well-being but also your self-esteem and self-worth. When you radiate confidence and self-assuredness, it naturally enhances your sexual magnetism and aligns you to frequencies of the same.

OPEN COMMUNICATION WITH YOUR PARTNER

Effective communication is the cornerstone of a satisfying sexual relationship, and meeting the Universe halfway could very well involve having an open and honest conversation with your partner about your desires, boundaries and fantasies. Creating a safe, non-judgemental space for these conversations allows both of you to better understand each other's needs and aspirations. By discussing your desires and boundaries openly, you create an environment in which you can explore new experiences together and grow as a couple.

CAN I MANIFEST A MARRIAGE PROPOSAL?

Yes, yes, a thousand times, yes. Begin by having a clear and specific vision of the kind of marriage you desire. Journal on questions such as what qualities do I want in a life partner? What balance do I desire within the household? What kind of relationship do I envision? What values are important to me? Clarity on your marriage sets the foundation for manifesting the perfect proposal. Here are some ideas for achieving the proposal of your dreams:

USE YOUR IMAGINATION

At this point, introduce visualization into your daily routine. Close your eyes and imagine your ideal proposal. Imagine seeing your partner's face opposite you. Create a movie in your mind, visualizing what they will say – and, more importantly, connecting to how you will feel in that moment. Think about the location, what you are wearing, what the ring looks like – visualizing smaller details like this helps to align your energy to your desired state.

MAKE A VISION BOARD

Having a visual representation of your desires can help reinforce your intentions by keeping them at the forefront of your mind, so why not pull together a vision board that represents your ideal marriage and proposal? Include images, quotes, colours, symbols, and so on, that resonate with your vision of what your desired partnership and proposal mean to you. Your vision board can be kept private as a digital board online, or perhaps out in the open for your partner to see if you're giving the Universe a helping hand.

RADIATE LOVE

One of the most powerful ways you can align to the energetic state of love, joy and happiness is to explore how you can put more of that out into the world. Cultivate feelings of love within yourself. Engage in activities that bring you joy, like spending time with loved ones and practising self-care. When we radiate positive energy out into the world, we attract similar vibrations, and I can almost guarantee your partner will feed off this energy.

SHOW GRATITUDE

Something to remember, not just while manifesting a marriage proposal but also throughout your relationship together, is to express gratitude for your partner. Consciously acknowledge and appreciate the qualities that you love about them, focusing on the positive aspects of your relationship, especially during times when this can feel challenging. This is where gratitude has the power to shift your energetic state to something that serves you better.

PREPARE FOR THE PROPOSAL

A really fun way to manifest a marriage proposal is to prep as if you already know it is happening. Act as if your marriage proposal is on its way, preparing in practical ways such as getting your nails done or making plans for your future wedding together. You could pre-write a social media announcement (just be careful not to accidentally post it) or a text message to your friends sharing the amazing news. Acting as if it is already yours puts you in the energy of assumption and sends a message to the Universe that you are confident and ready to receive.

LOOSEN YOUR GRIP ON THE OUTCOME

However, I do want to add a caveat here by noting that while it is essential to be clear about your desires, it's equally important not to strangle them and to allow yourself to detach from the outcome. The way I describe this is: you can't accept an engagement ring on your finger while your hand is gripping something tightly. Release your grip, extend your hand and be ready to say yes, yes, a thousand times, yes.

MONEY

I WANT TO MANIFEST MONEY. WHERE DO I START?

The truth is, I could write an entire book on the concept of manifesting money. In fact, there has been a wealth of books (excuse the pun) on this very subject over the years, from *Think and Grow Rich* by Napoleon Hill in 1937 to more recent examples like *You Are A Badass At Making Money* by Jen Sincero in 2017.

However, to condense manifesting money into a single chapter, let's begin by looking at it as a form of energy. Money is a neutral resource, neither negative nor positive. It is the thoughts and actions behind money that carry the attachment. For example, money can be used to buy weapons for war, but it can also be used to clear plastic from the ocean. The person who holds the money chooses the energy it carries and what values they align with.

Once you view money as a neutral resource, you can begin removing the attachments you have placed on it over the years. And I am certain you hold at least one negative belief around money. As we grow up, our beliefs about money are shaped by

the people around us – parents, guardians, friends, school, the media, and so on. If you grew up in an environment where money was scarce, where bills were a struggle, and where phrases like 'money is the root of all evil' and 'money doesn't grow on trees' were part of your everyday vocabulary, it is no wonder that it feels alien to believe we can attract money through our thoughts.

The generational beliefs that came from your parents were given to them by their parents, which were passed down from their parents, and so on. But you have the power to change this reality and stop the chain of money beliefs in its tracks. Before we move on to how to manifest money, we must break through any old beliefs that are blocking the route of abundance from flowing to you. Let's explore some common money beliefs that people have, as well as how to reframe these positively. By reframing, and consistently repeating these new beliefs, we can build new neural pathways in our minds and weaken the old negative ones.

REFRAMING YOUR MONEY MINDSET

Limiting Belief: 'I'm not good with money.'

Reframe: 'I am capable of learning and improving my financial skills. I am open to gaining knowledge and seeking guidance to make better financial decisions.'

Limiting Belief: 'I don't deserve to be wealthy.'

Reframe: 'I am deserving of abundance and success. My worth is not determined solely by my financial status, and I can create wealth while making a positive impact in the world.'

Limiting Belief: 'Rich people are greedy or selfish.'

Reframe: 'Wealthy individuals have the potential to make a positive difference in their communities and beyond. I can use my financial success to support causes I care about and inspire others to do the same.'

Limiting Belief: 'I'm afraid of failure or losing everything.'

Reframe: 'Failure is a natural part of growth and learning. Each setback brings me closer to success, and I am resilient enough to overcome challenges on my path to financial abundance.'

Limiting Belief: 'I need to work hard to earn money.'

Reframe: 'I can attract abundance by working smart and aligning my actions with my goals. I am open to receiving opportunities, wealth and success with ease and flow.'

Once you have established the state of your relationship with money and the nurturing it may need, it is time to get specific about the amount of money you would like to manifest. The Universe loves specificity, especially when it comes to money. For example, if your manifestation is to 'have more money', then you could find a penny on the street and have 'more' than you did the day before. But we both know that isn't what you meant by more money.

How much money would you like right now and, more importantly, what would you like it for? The question of 'what for' is important here because the Universe may very well deliver abundance in the shape of the thing you desire, rather than money in the bank.

My advice? If this is your first foray into manifesting money, start small. Let the goal feel exciting but not so much of a stretch that you can't visualize it ever happening. Start with £100, for example. Build your trust in the Universe. Imagine what it will feel like to have that money in your account and what it will allow you to do. Connect to the energy of what it feels like to have more money. Is it relief? Is it freedom? When you lean into this energy, that is when you become magnetic to your desires. You could write a Letter of Gratitude to the Universe as if you have already received the money you are manifesting, and share what you used it for and how it made you feel. You could sign a blank cheque from the Universe and carry it with you.

Finally, release any ideas of how and when the money will arrive. Because if there's anything I've learned over the years of manifesting hundreds of thousands of pounds into my life, it's that the Universe will choose the most weird, wonderful and unexpected routes for abundance to flow. Throughout this chapter, I will share some of those stories, as well as other tips and tricks for manifesting more money into your life.

WHAT ARE SOME DAILY HABITS TO HELP ME MANIFEST MORE MONEY?

Now you are familiar with the basic concept of manifesting money – release, ask, believe, receive – let's explore some rituals that you can embrace to allow more abundance to flow into your life.

CHECK YOUR BANK ACCOUNT DAILY

Are you afraid to check your bank account? If so, you are in a state of lack and fear. When we are tuned into that energetic frequency, we attract more reasons to feel lack. Checking in daily alerts you to money going out, but also potential money coming in. Every time you check your bank account, you are confronting any attached fears, and those old negative patterns can slowly but surely be released. You are taking back control.

CREATE ANCHORS

Anchors are physical or mental cues that can help you reconnect to the feeling of abundance, triggering an emotional response. For example:

Scent A beautifully fragranced candle can evoke a feeling of abundance throughout your house, as can a perfume that makes you feel like your vision-board self.

Numbers Change the passcode on your phone to the amount of money you'd like to manifest, so you are reminded of this figure throughout the day, until it no longer feels out of reach.

Music Create an Abundance playlist with songs that increase your vibrations and remind you of the endless possibilities available to us. Better still, move stagnant energy in your body by dancing to this playlist each day.

Texture An anchor that worked incredibly well when I began my money manifesting journey was purchasing a single silk pillowcase, which helped me imagine what life would feel like when I was abundant enough to own the entire bed set.

MONEY MANTRAS
A money mantra is an empowering phrase or affirmation that you repeat to yourself regularly to cultivate a healthy and abundant mindset around money. The key is to stay consistent and repeat daily to see noticeable shifts in your mindset.

BE EXPECTANT
Imagine receiving a phone call to inform you a large sum of money is on its way to you, but it will take a few weeks to clear in your account. How would you feel? I imagine your vibrations would be skyrocketing, right?

Can you see how, even though you haven't received any money yet, your energy has shifted? This is how the most powerful manifestors live – in the energy of expectancy. You feel drawn to manifest something because it is already out in the world and available for you. The sooner you move into the energy of expecting it to be yours, the quicker the Universe can conspire to make it yours in the physical realm.

CONNECT WITH CRYSTALS

By focusing on your desire for financial abundance while holding or meditating with certain crystals, you amplify the energy you're putting out into the Universe. Here are three crystals to attract more abundance into your life.

Citrine: Known as the 'Merchant's Stone', citrine is believed to enhance motivation and creativity and produce positive energy.

Pyrite: Also known as 'Fool's Gold', pyrite is thought to attract wealth, prosperity and success.

Green aventurine: This heart-centred crystal is often associated with luck, opportunity and wealth. It's believed to bring positive outcomes in financial matters and enhance a sense of personal power.

MONEY MANTRA EXAMPLES

- Money flows easily and effortlessly.
- My mindset is a magnet for wealth, and every positive thought I have attracts more money to me.
- I am open to receiving abundance in whichever way the Universe chooses to deliver it.

Q

CAN I MANIFEST MYSELF OUT OF DEBT?

Yes, you can. I say this with such conviction because
I manifested myself out of £20,000-plus worth of debt in
my early 30s. While I would always recommend reaching out
to a financial specialist for help if you are struggling to manage
any debt you have acquired, I do want to share the mindset
behind releasing debt, which can help you move from a feeling
of scarcity and fear to one of abundance and control.

You may spot throughout this chapter that I purposely craft
the language used, such as 'releasing debt', instead of 'being in
debt', and 'I chose not to invest in that' rather than 'I couldn't
afford it'. That's because the language we use around money is
incredibly powerful. Debt should not be seen as a negative. It
is simply a way of paying for something in instalments, a way
of accessing something you need while spreading the payment
over a particular time period. When businesses use credit, it is
called leveraging, but over the years there has been a negative
attachment placed on personal use. It is time to release any
shame and guilt you have attached to using credit cards, loans
and overdrafts.

TAKE BACK CONTROL

You are in the driver's seat now when it comes to releasing debt. Embrace this challenge and get a full and clear picture of your financial situation. Remove your head from the sand. Write down and acknowledge every single dime that is outstanding and make moving out of debt your intention for the next year (or however long it may take).

As soon as I took back control and challenged myself to pay off small amounts of debt each month, the Universe could finally begin to deliver abundance to me in expected and unexpected ways. It's fair to say that once I began paying money towards the debt I had, focusing on the small amounts first and celebrating every time I saw those numbers going down, I became addicted to the feeling of joy and achievement it brought.

While I created an achievable budget from my 9-to-5 monthly wage at the time, I also began to actively tune into downloads and nudges from the Universe – guiding me to the aligned action I needed to take to welcome more money in. These nudges could look like selling old clothes on a secondhand site, trading in your old tech, sharing your skills online, taking part in market research, following up with an old contact about potential freelance work, leaving reviews of products, cutting the lawn for your neighbours, working Saturdays in a bookstore – there are a plethora of possibilities available when you tune into where the Universe might be leading you.

MULTIPLE PAYMENTS

You may be wondering, 'But can I not just manifest a large sum of money and wipe out the debt in one go?' The answer would be: absolutely. Set the intention, visualize how that would feel, and release the desire ready to receive in divine timing. However, don't forget: the Universe could still deliver your desired amount, but in smaller chunks over time. I received £800 bonuses, £2,000 inheritance from a relative, £1,500 payment from extra work, an unexpected £5,000 refund from a loan I had taken out ten years prior. The list goes on.

FINANCIAL FREEDOM

Celebrate every time you make a dent in your tally. Every time you tick off a milestone. Every time you go to spend money without thinking, but purposely choose to put it towards your financially free, empowered life instead. Every time you visualize what life could be like without the heaviness you have carried with you for this long.

HOW CAN I FEEL ABUNDANT WHEN MY REALITY REFLECTS THE OPPOSITE?

Repeat after me: abundance is a state of mind, rather than an amount in the bank. Abundance is the way we feel, the energy with which we approach life, the way we focus on what we have rather than what is missing.

Yet the art of detachment and holding our faith, especially when it comes to manifesting money, can be one of the most difficult practices to execute. It can feel especially hard when bills are due and you are wondering when the next pay cheque will come to help feed your family.

I do remember how frustrated I felt when I first read somewhere that being broke is simply a state of mind. My lived experience said that being without money was a very valid and real part of my life – where no amount of mindset could change the fact that I had 27p with which to find some lunch before payday. But I can also now see how comfortable I felt in survival mode. Having money felt unnatural to me, which meant that every time financial abundance came into my life,

I would either actively spend it or unconsciously sabotage my growth by attracting a large bill, usually matching the exact amount of spare money I had.

One of the first mindset shifts I made was to change the direction of money in my mind. While in reality it felt as if every time money came into my life, it would flow right back out, I decided to – almost delusionally – believe that each time I paid a bill, money would come back to me tenfold.

Delusion or not, ever since I chose this state of mind when paying my bills each month, focusing on what those bills have enabled me to have and consistently repeating the mantra 'Every time I pay money out, it returns to me tenfold', my bank account has continued to experience an overflow of financial abundance. Not millions. But an overflow of money that allows me to live a life I truly love.

LOOK FOR FINANCIAL POSITIVES
Another piece of advice is to consider your consumption of media. If you are constantly being fed the narrative that money is scarce, shares are plummeting and the economy is in turmoil, it's no wonder you feel resistance to attracting abundance into your life. Look for where money is being spent, made and celebrated in a positive way. New businesses that have opened. Charities that are thriving. Lottery winners.

BE GRATEFUL
The most important mindset shift you can embrace when you're in a state of fear and lack is gratitude. For the money you have physically. For the money available to you if you need it. For the money you have already received and what it has enabled you to have, do and be.

In a gratitude journal write down the small, big and magical moments of abundance you experience throughout the day, from money you found in an old handbag to the quiet carriage you found yourself in on the train. Maybe your neighbour cut some flowers from their garden and brought them over, or you grabbed the last of the bread, meaning you could make one of your epic sandwiches for lunch. Remember, abundance isn't just an amount in your bank account, it is a state of mind.

BE GENEROUS

Finally, give without expecting anything in return and watch how the Universe rewards you. While it might sound counterintuitive to give away money when it is the one thing you want to attract, know that by giving – even if it is leaving a small amount somewhere for someone to find or making a donation to a charity close to your heart – you will create a cosmic boomerang effect and what you give out will return in equal value or more.

Q

I FEEL LIKE MY DREAM LIFE ISN'T POSSIBLE WITHOUT MANIFESTING MILLIONS. WHERE DO I START?

One of the first exercises I ask my clients to do is to calculate what they need for their dream life. Why? Because it is a common misconception that we need millions in the bank to live our dream life – or what we first assume our dream life to be, at least. For the majority of people, that simply isn't the case.

Take your journal and write down everything you'd like in your life each month to fulfil your soul. Think of this as the dream budget you'll have as your vision-board self. There are no limitations or restrictions. However, stay clear of plucking arbitrary numbers from thin air – this task is designed to help you see how close you could be to living your dream life right now.

Find out the estimated cost of each item on your list to create a dream life budget. If the life you dream about sees you having a gardener twice a month, research online how much a local gardener in your area costs and add that to your list. If you desire a weekly food delivery service, look online to see how much it would cost to feed your household.

EXAMPLES OF WHAT YOUR DREAM LIFE LIST COULD INCLUDE:

Financial and Essential Expenses: Rent/mortgage, Bills (utilities, internet, phone), Car expenses (payments, insurance, fuel, maintenance)

Self-care and Well-being: Gym membership/personal trainer, Massages and beauty treatments, Spiritual self-care items such as crystals and reiki sessions

Household and Convenience: Cleaner service, Gardener, Laundry/ironing, Food delivery, Extra groceries for special occasions or treats

Dining and Entertainment: Eating out at restaurants, Leisure activities (cinema, coffee outings, subscriptions to TV apps, books, events and shows, etc.)

Family and Children: Purchases for children's needs and interests

Travel and Experiences: Allocating funds for a holiday, Saving for future travel

Personal Style: Budget for updating your wardrobe or buying new clothes

Long-term Planning: Contributions to retirement and savings accounts, Investments for building wealth and financial security

Spiritual and Mindfulness: Budget for spiritual growth and practices (books, workshops, retreats)

Education and Learning: Funds for personal development courses or workshops

Giving Back: Allocations for charitable donations or volunteering initiatives

Remember, this is your blueprint for a dream life and no one else's. Leave comparison and social media status at the door please. If you find yourself asking, 'Do I crave this just for external validation?', then consider if it really is a good addition to your dream life budget.

How much does your dream life cost? Perhaps this monthly budget is £5,000 a month? Perhaps it's £50,000 a month? The reason calculating your dream life is so important is because it shines a light on what changes would lead to a happier life. Once you have this information, you can begin to see where you might be able to budget, and so incorporate some of this magic in the now. For example, if you have a personal trainer in your dream life, have you considered halving the cost with a friend once a week? Or have you looked at a monthly membership to the cinema that allows you to go as often as you like with one payment? Perhaps buying one new crystal a month would satisfy your spiritual needs, meaning you could swap your weekly coffee in your current budget to allow for that?

I'm not saying that the simple act of calculating your dream life makes it possible overnight, but bringing awareness and tangible figures to the mix can make it feel more real. Plus, we know the Universe appreciates specificity when it comes to manifesting money – let's see how these desires begin to show up in your life now you have set the intention to welcome them in.

CAN I MANIFEST FREE THINGS AND GIFTS?

You can manifest anything. Gifts, a bunch of flowers, free coffees, parking spaces. In fact, these can be some of the easiest things to manifest because there's usually very little attachment to the outcome. Of course, free things are nice. A parking space is great. Flowers delivered? Amazing. But do you have a deep-rooted limiting belief that you are not worthy of a parking space? Perhaps not so much. There is less resistance to work through. Which is why being in the energy of receiving gifts from the Universe can be a great way to start your manifesting journey.

The key is to affirm to yourself that you manifest free things easily. What evidence do you have that the Universe delivers magic into your life? I can guarantee that you receive gifts and free things throughout your day, but you haven't quite noticed. Someone holding the lift for you. Your colleague grabbing you a glass of water as they go to fill up their own. An old book a friend passed on that you've been meaning to read. All of these are gifts from the Universe that we're often blind to. And once you embrace gratitude for those small moments, the Universe can deliver more to be grateful for.

Be in the energy of expectancy. I always expect to get the parking space that I desire. I assume that I'll receive a free hot chocolate every now and then. I am open to receiving flowers whatever way they come.

I appreciate all of the small, beautiful moments of magic throughout the day, and with that energy of thankfulness, I magnetize more back in return. I am a person who receives gifts.

Can you see how that dialogue affirms the energy that I'm willing to receive? There's no hesitation or apologizing for my desires. It is also another reminder of how careful we need to be when repeating language such as 'I never win anything' or 'I'm just not a lucky person' – the more we affirm this, the more it becomes our reality.

Here's to manifesting small moments of magic into every day – especially the perfect parking spot. Nothing quite beats that feeling.

WHAT GIFT OR FREE THING WOULD YOU LIKE TO MANIFEST RIGHT NOW?

Let's use flowers as an example. Ask the Universe, either out loud or perhaps by writing the intention in your journal. Visualize a beautiful bunch of flowers sitting in your home, imagining how you'll feel looking at this beautiful gift. Maybe add a picture of some flowers to your desk so you see them daily. Take inspired action by making sure you have a vase suitable. And finally, release the intention to the Universe and trust that your flowers will arrive, and in the meantime, lean into gratitude for all that you already have in life.

HOW DO I ACT AS IF I ALREADY HAVE THE WEALTH I DESIRE SO THAT I AM AN ENERGETIC MATCH FOR IT?

Here are 50 ways you can move into the energy of abundance:

1. Dress for the life you desire. Wear clothes that make you feel abundant and declutter anything not aligned to your vision.
2. Choose high-quality, nourishing foods where possible.
3. Practise random acts of kindness and generosity.
4. Clear out physical and mental clutter to make space for abundance.
5. Appreciate the changes in the seasons.
6. Practise mindfulness and meditation.
7. Create a playlist of uplifting and positive songs.
8. Read books on abundance, success and wealth.
9. Document your manifestations in a journal as if they've already occurred.

10. Research and plan a dream holiday.

11. Find a signature fragrance that makes you feel wealthy.

12. Treat yourself to a luxurious bath or spa day at home.

13. Create a ritual around making great coffee each morning.

14. Invest in luxurious bedding for a better night's sleep.

15. Surround yourself with supportive and positive people.

16. Test drive your dream car.

17. Cultivate a beautiful garden or some indoor plants.

18. Treat yourself to a fancy dinner and visualize this being a regular occurrence.

19. Enhance your living space with small new decorative items.

20. Display photos of your dream travel destinations.

21. Invest in art that makes you feel abundant when you look at it.

22. Wear jewellery that makes you feel wealthy.

23. Use essential oils associated with abundance, such as patchouli and ylang ylang.

24. Use a financial planner or app to track your progress.

25. Invest in a luxurious bathrobe.

26. Study the habits of successful people who you admire.

27. Give back to your community through volunteering and access the energy of a philanthropist.

28. Practise deep, mindful breathing.

29. Prioritize a restful night's sleep.

30. Learn about abundance and manifestation from experts.

31. Enjoy herbal teas associated with abundance like chamomile or mint.

32. Curate a playlist of songs that inspire success.

33. Apply feng shui principles to your living space to attract positive energy (see page 149).

34. Write about how your life has been transformed since you manifested the financial abundance you desire.

35. Plan a beautiful staycation at home, researching local routes to walk and activities that you have been meaning to try.

36. Carry a crystal or stone that represents abundance.

37. Watch films or documentaries about financial success.

38. Read books on cultivating an abundance mindset.

39. Treat yourself to a beautiful bunch of flowers.

40. Trial free things to help you access how it would feel if they were your reality.

41. Try cooking a gourmet meal at home.

42. Plan special outings or activities with loved ones.

43. Place positive affirmations on mirrors in your home.

44. Listen to podcasts on wealth-building.

45. Design a morning routine that starts your day with abundance, such as writing in your gratitude journal.

46. Arrange a photoshoot to capture your most abundant self.

47. Share your journey on social media and connect with like-minded individuals.

48. Take walks in nature while focusing on your financial goals.

49. Write thank-you notes to the Universe for your manifestations.

50. Perform rituals or intentions during the full moon to amplify the energy of abundance.

CAREER

HOW DO I MANIFEST A NEW JOB?

Regardless of whether you're still drawn to your childhood dream job or have discovered new passions as you've grown older, doing something you enjoy while being paid for it is a magical combination. But before you send your desire into the Universe, let's nail down the specifics of the job you want to manifest into your life. For example:

- What industry do you want to work in?
- Do you want to work alone or as part of a team?
- What salary would you like?
- Do you want to work remotely or commute to the office?
- How do you want to feel in your role? Appreciated? Supported? Motivated? Balanced?
- What daily tasks would you like to do?

The reason we specify the smaller details, rather than asking the Universe for a specific role, is that something may come along that has everything you desire but a different job title to the one that you asked for in your original manifestation request.

INSPIRED ACTION

Now you have your cosmic shopping list of specifics, what inspired action can you take towards manifesting your dream role? The first piece of inspired action is making

sure your CV is up to date. How would the vision-board version of you show up on their CV? I'm betting they don't shy away from their achievements. Future you – the version of you that already has their dream role – is proud and confident in their abilities and isn't afraid to share them with others.

Be sure to tell others about your dream role and that you are actively manifesting it. By speaking your goals into existence with others, you're opening new routes for the Universe to deliver. For example, a friend could know of a position that has just become available. Or a family member might recommend a contact who is happy to mentor you.

This is where saying yes is pivotal. If you are asked into a meeting, go. If you are asked for lunch, go. If a contact reaches out to connect via LinkedIn, send a message to say hello. If you feel pulled to visit the careers section of a certain website, follow that nudge. As with manifesting anything, the Universe may lead you with gentle nudges and at other times with a cartoon-style frying pan around the head!

RELEASING DOUBT

At this point, you may have that niggling voice in your head, your inner critic, listing all the reasons why you're *not* suitable for your dream job, or why it could never be yours. Can you find evidence to counter those beliefs? Ask your subconscious to find reasons why you *are* suitable for the role and see what it reaches for. You have a 100 per cent success rate of overcoming everything that has been thrown at you thus far in life, so, as far as the Universe is concerned, you're more than qualified.

THE POWER OF VISUALIZATION

What happens when – not if – you find your dream role, apply and then secure the interview? Here, visualization is your best friend. Imagine the feeling of sitting in the interview, with calm energy, knowing you have an answer to every question asked. Create a film in your mind where you are sitting with the team, getting along swimmingly and aligned in energy – they want you just as much as you want this role. Make this visualization so clear and lifelike, tapping into that potent energy of it being yours already, that the subconscious has no idea whether this is your reality or imagination.

Moving out of the imagination and into the now, let's explore how you could align yourself to the energy of the person who has been offered this dream job. How would you dress? What would your first-day outfit be? What route would you take to work? Where would you grab lunch or your morning coffee? Go there and imagine you are on your break. Pre-write your letter of resignation. Visualize getting the phone call to say the job is yours – how does that energy feel? Exciting, I imagine!

EXPRESS GRATITUDE

Finally, as you release your grip on the 'how' and 'when', letting the Universe work its magic, can you move into an energy of gratitude for your current role? While I completely understand toxic work environments (more on that in the next question on page 92), being in an energy of unhappiness, frustration and anger is challenging when you want to align to the frequency of a new, exciting and inspiring role. Which is where gratitude comes into play.

What can you be grateful for? Is it the commute that enables you to listen to your favourite podcast before work? Or is there a local park nearby that you get to visit every lunchtime during summer. Maybe you get along really well with a certain team member and you can be grateful for their energy. Find mini moments of gratitude each day to help guide you through this transition period.

MANIFESTING TIP

While it is a great idea to apply for more than one job vacancy – you allow your manifestation to breathe this way, rather than putting all of your focus on one thing – applying for anything and everything is a sign of a frantic energy of lack. Take your foot off the pedal for just a moment and reassess where you can be a little more intentional. Don't waste your time (and the Universe's) applying for jobs that you already know in your gut aren't aligned to your overall vision.

I WORK IN A TOXIC ENVIRONMENT. CAN THE UNIVERSE HELP ME WITH THIS?

Many of us, myself included, have experienced a toxic work environment. It can range from bullying and experiencing microaggressions to passive-aggressive emails, sitting in a heavy atmosphere or feeling unheard and unappreciated, to name just a few examples.

My first piece of advice when it comes to working in a toxic environment is to look for alternative employment, but this isn't always possible. My second piece of advice is: do not water the plants of negativity. Sometimes it can feel as if the only option you have is to match people where they are on the emotional scale, but adding more negativity to this environment will only damage your energetic frequency.

You are in control of your energy; do not outsource that control to someone else. How can you lean into understanding? What are you choosing to focus on throughout the day? How can you kill people (figuratively speaking, of course) with kindness? I promise, rising above someone else's negative energy will always serve you better in the long run.

PROTECTION BUBBLE VISUALIZATION

In times of stress and negativity, it's important to protect your energy and well-being. Visualization techniques can be a powerful tool to help you maintain your inner peace and resilience, especially in a toxic work environment. This visualization exercise will guide you in creating a protective energy bubble around yourself to shield against negativity and maintain your positive mindset.

Step 1 Choose a quiet and comfortable place where you can sit or lie down in a relaxed position, with your spine straight and hands resting comfortably in your lap.

Step 2 Take a few deep breaths to centre yourself. Inhale slowly through your nose, counting to four, and then exhale through your mouth, again counting to four.

CRYSTALS TO HAVE ON YOUR DESK

Black tourmaline: This is an excellent crystal for grounding and protection. It can help shield you from negative energies and promote a sense of security.

Selenite: Known for its cleansing and purifying properties, selenite can help clear your mind and create a peaceful atmosphere, aiding you in maintaining a sense of calm and mental clarity amid workplace turmoil.

Blue lace agate: A soothing crystal that promotes clear communication and tranquillity, blue lace agate can help you to express yourself effectively while keeping a level head in challenging workplace interactions.

Step 3 Close your eyes and imagine roots extending from the soles of your feet deep into the Earth. Visualize these roots anchoring you.

Step 4 Imagine a bubble of light surrounding your entire body. This bubble is a powerful shield that will protect you from any negative energy or toxicity in your work environment.

Step 5 Choose the colour of your protective bubble – a colour that resonates with you and represents protection and positivity. It could be white, gold or any colour that feels right to you.

Step 6 Affirm to yourself that this bubble will only allow positive energy to enter and will protect you from negativity. Say to yourself, 'I am safe and protected within this bubble. Only love and positivity can enter, and negativity is repelled.'

Step 7 Visualize this bubble growing stronger and brighter with each breath you take. Imagine it expanding to include your workspace, colleagues and any other elements of your work environment.

Step 8 When you're ready, slowly open your eyes and return to the present moment. Carry the feeling of your protective bubble with you as you go about your day, knowing that you have the tools to shield yourself from toxicity. Throughout your workday, whenever you encounter negativity or toxicity, return to this visualization. Reinforce your protective bubble by taking a moment to breathe deeply and visualize it becoming even stronger.

HOW DO I CALL IN SOULMATE CLIENTS AND CUSTOMERS?

Calling in a soulmate client or customer is a lot like calling in a soulmate love. What characteristics do you desire in this person? How do you want to feel around them? Do you want someone who takes action? Maybe you want someone open-minded and willing to try something new. If you're a hairdresser, for example, your dream client could be someone who is so happy with their new haircut that they share online and tag your business with great feedback.

Working as a coach, for example, my soulmate client is open to both manifestation and mindset tools, happy to embrace spirituality and science. They are excited to invest in their future. They put the action into the Law of Attraction. They give great feedback and happily share their experience of working with me online. They turn up to calls on time. They come to our calls prepared, with things to share and questions to ask. I'm extremely lucky to say the Universe delivers souls like this to me time and time again.

The real question, however, is: are you embodying the energy you want to attract? For example, if you want your invoices paid on time, yet you're continually late paying yours, how can you expect to magnetize the opposite of what you're putting out? You are saying to the Universe that it is okay to pay bills late.

If you never leave a review of a small business, how can you expect people to leave a review for yours? If you seldom reply to comments on Instagram, why would people open a line of communication on yours? Can you see how the energy you're putting out is the energy being magnetized back to you?

Have you created routes for the Universe to deliver soulmate clients to the business? One of the ways I would sabotage my success when I first began in business was to have broken links on my website. Yes, someone could visit my website and see if they felt aligned, but as soon as they tried to contact me, the link didn't work. Can you believe that? Even when a friend pointed this out, I still took months to fix it. That was until I did the inner work on my fear of success and realized what a difference I could make to people's lives if I cleared the blocks (both energetic and literal).

JOURNAL PROMPTS

How can I embody the characteristics of my soulmate client/customer?

How can I understand my soulmate client better?

How can I infuse my brand with qualities my soulmate client is attracted to?

How can I show gratitude to the soulmate clients I already have?

Make it easy for people to purchase things from you. Create clear routes. What confusion do you need to untangle in your business right now? Put your lights on. Share what your product/service/offer is.

Saying yes to everyone and everything because of financial fear, however, moves you into an energy of scarcity and lack. And when we're vibrating at the frequency of lack, we magnetize more reasons to feel lack – such as unaligned clients. Clients and customers that add stress to the business. Who don't pay invoices on time. Who turn up late. Who don't appreciate your work.

To move out of this energy, focus on the people who are an amazing fit for your business. Maybe you already have someone who you regard as a soulmate client – how about sending them a personal note to let them know how thankful you are for them? How can you show gratitude for the people who have chosen to follow your journey? Change your focus from what you are lacking to those small moments of magic you can be grateful for.

I DIDN'T GET THE DREAM JOB
I THOUGHT I'D MANIFESTED.
WHAT HAPPENED?

At the age of 23, fresh out of university and with big dreams about moving to the big city, I would have described my dream job as working in the fashion cupboard for a national magazine, filling my days with beautiful clothes, photoshoots and writing articles. I applied for a role that ticked all of the boxes on my cosmic shopping list. It felt divinely sent.

I was certain that the job was mine. Roles like this didn't come around very often and there it was, waiting for me to apply. The interview went well – I thought I'd made a great impression. The team laughed at my jokes, they were impressed with the portfolio of freelance work I'd amassed, and they told me how much they'd enjoyed the fashion blog I had been writing behind the scenes. The energy felt right. There I was, an eager young graduate, ready to make the move into the world of fashion.

Except...I didn't get the job. When the email came to say they had gone with someone else, I didn't quite believe it at first.

I thought it might have been sent to me by mistake. That's how confident I was about getting this job. It was like the Universe had presented this amazing opportunity and then snatched it out of my hands. I felt rejected.

NOT THIS, BUT SOMETHING BETTER

When I didn't get that longed-for job, however, I wasn't being rejected. I was being redirected. Redirected to something bigger and better. More than I could ever imagine. Because two months later, I was offered the role of Acting Editor of a fashion magazine, which then led to me spending a decade as Editor-in-Chief. This role had everything on my cosmic shopping list and also some added bonuses that I didn't quite realize I craved at the time. The Universe was keeping me from the fashion cupboard, so that I could sit on the front row at fashion shows.

Perhaps you didn't get this dream job of yours because something better suited is coming. Something that you can't even comprehend right now. Maybe something with a better salary. Or an easier commute. With a better team of people around you or flexible hours to suit your lifestyle.

Maybe the Universe was keeping you from that 'dream role' because of stressors we can't see on the surface. On paper, it seemed like everything you desired, and yet in reality it was far from that. What can you take away from this situation? Are there any lessons or teachings you can take away from the interview process? Do you need to alter your cosmic shopping list to suit your new manifestation?

A client I worked with to manifest her dream job was despondent when her original interview didn't go as planned, and yet a month later the same company came back to say they had created a role specifically for her. The dream job didn't come along the route she imagined and, without sounding like a broken record, this is why releasing the 'how' and 'when' is so important when it comes to manifestation.

Continue to look for those signs, listen to nudges, and trust that the Universe got your order the first time you asked. Your dream role is on its way. Your manifestation wants you, just as much as you want it. Give it time. Only in hindsight will you see how divine timing was at play. Don't keep going into the kitchen to check on the chef to see if your food is ready. Instead, sit and enjoy the restaurant and the company around you, safe in the knowledge that your order will arrive when it's perfectly cooked.

HOW CAN I MANIFEST A BETTER WORK-LIFE BALANCE?

The elusive journey to create a better balance between work and life. Is such a thing possible? I believe so. But it takes awareness and boundaries. Life flows in seasons and while some seasons will be busier than others, it is up to us to make sure that slowing down, and being mindful of the moment we're in, is non-negotiable.

The first step in creating more balance in our every day is acknowledging what balance actually means to you:

Is it deleting the email app on your phone over the weekend?

Is it leaving work at your contracted time?

Is it having the energy to be able to spend time with your family?

Is it having regular digital detoxes, taking a break from social media entirely?

Is it embracing a much slower pace of life overall?

For some, these things may seem like a given. But for many, in our fast-paced, driven, career-focused society where hustle is celebrated and overtime is expected, this can feel like a pipe dream.

It is also worth noting that when it comes to work-life balance, it is important to recognize where your ego may be playing a role. The concept of the ego is primarily associated with Sigmund Freud's psychoanalytic theory of personality. In Freud's model, the ego is one of the three major components of the mind, along with the id and the superego. Think of the id as the impulsive and instinctual part of your mind that focuses on immediate gratification of your desires and needs. It doesn't care about consequences or what's socially acceptable – it wants what it wants, when it wants it. The superego is your moral compass or your conscience, representing the rules, norms and values of society that you've internalized.

MANIFESTATION TIP

While this might be a stretch for the sceptical readers among you, you can quite literally ask the Universe for more time. Once you do, you may begin to notice that you have manifested a better flow of work or meetings being cancelled, or feel a sense of calmness that allows you to get work finished without feeling flustered. Try it the next time you are in a state of overwhelm.

THE ROLE OF THE EGO

The ego's role in the work-life balance is complex as it can influence your behaviour in several ways:

Identity and Self-Esteem: The ego plays a significant role in shaping our identity and self-esteem. Success and achievement at work can boost self-esteem, leading many of us to prioritize work over other aspects of life as a means of bolstering our ego.

Social Comparisons: Ego can drive us to compare ourselves to others, especially in terms of career accomplishments. This competitive mindset may lead us to overwork in an attempt to outperform our peers.

Fear of Failure and Perfectionism: An ego-driven fear of failure or desire for perfectionism can make it difficult for many of us to disconnect from work. We may feel any time spent away from work is wasted or that we must continuously prove ourselves.

Once you recognize the role of ego in your journey toward a more balanced approach to work, you can begin to do the inner work needed to make positive changes. For example, if you acknowledge that your identity has been shaped by your career, a powerful journal prompt is to ask five people closest to you what your superpowers are. What makes you, you, in this world. Notice what is said, aside from your career.

Next, begin to think about how 'future you' spends their time now they have more balance between work and home. Schedule those ideas in your diary. Embody that version of you in the present day. Stick to plans at home just as you would a meeting at work. By acting as if you already have a more balanced approach, you become a magnet to opportunities that allow for even more balance.

HOW CAN I MANIFEST A PROMOTION?

The energy behind manifesting a promotion is very similar to the one needed to manifest your dream job. Listen to nudges and directions from the Universe and say yes more often. Become the version of you that already has the promotion. How does that version of you show up each day? What do they wear? How do they approach meetings and have their voice heard? In the same way that you manifested your dream role, speak your desires into existence around you. Let people know you are looking to move up the career ladder.

'ISN'T IT WONDERFUL' TECHNIQUE

This is a great point in the book to introduce the 'Isn't It Wonderful' manifestation technique – a technique that many associate with Law of Attraction teacher Neville Goddard, thanks to his consistent use of the phrase in his teachings. This technique is designed to help you move to the final energetic state of how you will feel when your manifestation becomes reality, by repeating the phrase 'Isn't It Wonderful…' and then describing parts of your manifestation as if it were already your reality. For example, in this instance, 'Isn't it wonderful…

SOME 'ISN'T IT WONDERFUL...' AFFIRMATIONS

- Isn't it wonderful...that I now have the role of my dreams!
- Isn't it wonderful...that I'm earning double what I earned when I began at this company!
- Isn't it wonderful...that I'm working with an amazing team!
- Isn't it wonderful...that my experience has been acknowledged by my manager!
- Isn't it wonderful...that I get to sink my teeth into something new!
- Isn't it wonderful...that my dedication and hard work have paid off!
- Isn't it wonderful...that I've reached a new level of success in my career!
- Isn't it wonderful...that I'm now in a position to make a greater impact!
- Isn't it wonderful...that I have the opportunity to lead and inspire others!
- Isn't it wonderful...that I'm stepping into a more challenging and rewarding role!
- Isn't it wonderful...that my skills and expertise are being recognized and valued!
- Isn't it wonderful...that I'm on the path to even greater achievements!
- Isn't it wonderful...that I'm now part of the decision-making process in the company!
- Isn't it wonderful...that my career is flourishing and I'm achieving my goals!
- Isn't it wonderful...that I'm creating a brighter future for myself and my loved ones!

that my boss recognized my skills and promoted me'. Or 'Isn't it wonderful… that I get to be part of the management team where my ideas are heard and appreciated'.

At the core of Goddard's teachings is feeling as if your desires have already been fulfilled and living in a state of gratitude for those desires. The phrase 'Isn't It Wonderful' affirms to your subconscious – which isn't able to differentiate between reality and imagination – that your desires have come to fruition. In turn, this influences your behaviour and actions in a positive way as you manifest your promotion at work. Those behavioural changes could include putting yourself forward for extra responsibilities, feeling confident enough to book a meeting with your boss to discuss your future, or adding additional skills to your CV by signing up for an online course.

Is this a written or spoken exercise? Both are suitable but from experience, regularly speaking your desires into existence has a form of energetic magic that can't be replicated by sitting and writing in a journal. Plus, the beauty of speaking your desires out loud is that you can literally do it anywhere you feel comfortable – in the shower in the morning, in the car driving to work or even before bed. A multitasking manifestation technique at its finest. See previous page for more examples of 'Isn't It Wonderful' affirmations.

Q

I WANT TO DO MULTIPLE THINGS WITH MY LIFE, BUT WON'T THAT CONFUSE THE UNIVERSE?

Being multifaceted is one of the most beautiful and intriguing aspects of the human experience. It's a reflection of the ever-evolving nature of our lives, where we continually set new goals, cultivate different desires, and are drawn towards new experiences. The ability to embrace a multitude of dreams is, in itself, a privilege that we shouldn't take for granted.

From our childhood dreams to our adult ambitions, we are constantly evolving as individuals. We start with one set of goals, and as we grow and learn, our dreams change and expand. However, this multifaceted approach to life isn't without its sceptics and doubters. Some wonder whether pursuing multiple dreams and desires at once might confuse the Universe or dilute our focus. Is it possible, they ask, to effectively manifest more than one thing simultaneously? Can you truly manifest your dream job while also attracting clients for your passion project on the side? Is it possible to manifest new clients for an existing business while simultaneously pursuing a book deal for an idea you've nurtured for years?

These questions reflect the common manifestation myth that focusing solely on one goal at a time is the most effective way to achieve it. However, the reality is quite the opposite. Embracing our multifaceted nature can make us incredibly effective manifestors. Instead of fixating on a single outcome and constricting our desires with a tight grip on the 'how' and 'when', we learn the art of juggling our focus – and in turn, letting our manifestations breathe.

One of the positives of this multifaceted approach is adaptability. In today's ever-shifting world, where industries evolve and companies can change overnight, being able to wear different hats and navigate various fields becomes an amazing asset to have. When you are open to pursuing multiple passions and interests, you position yourself to seize opportunities as the Universe sees fit to deliver them.

Being multifaceted allows you to cast a wider net into the sea of possibilities. You can cast your desires like a net into the ocean, and as you draw it back in, you might just find a

diverse catch of experiences, achievements and opportunities. Embracing your multifaceted nature doesn't dilute your focus, but rather enhances it by allowing you to explore all that life has to offer.

The Universe is not limited by human concepts of time and space. It doesn't get confused or overwhelmed when you set multiple intentions. Instead, it responds to the energy and intention you infuse into each desire. The key is to maintain clarity and focus on each goal while allowing flexibility in how they unfold. Trust that the Universe has its own way of orchestrating events to align with your intentions.

Dare to dream big, set multiple intentions in your career and business, and watch as the Universe unfolds its magic in the most unexpected and delightful ways.

FRIENDS
AND
FAMILY

HOW CAN I MANIFEST MORE FRIENDSHIPS INTO MY LIFE?

No matter what season of life you find yourself in, no matter what box you tick in the age category, friendships can be tough to navigate. Perhaps you find yourself in a new city, or you've drifted apart from school friends as you chase different dreams. Maybe you're a new parent without anyone you can relate to, or you're child-free and craving adventure while everyone around you is married and planning baby number two.

Regardless of your current status, manifesting soul-aligned friendships into your life is absolutely possible. I have manifested an abundance of beautiful friendships over the years – ones that light me up and ones that offer me the opportunity to support, while also feeling equally supported. Ones that make me laugh until my stomach hurts. Ones with people who believe in my dreams more than I do. Ones with people who enjoy adventure. And ones with people who love a boxset binge and a large pizza.

But what exactly is a soul-aligned friendship? A soul-aligned friendship is a feeling of balance. You both give and take in equal measure. You leave your friend's company feeling uplifted, rather than depleted. You feel seen, heard and understood.

Have you ever had a friendship with someone that has left you feeling 'less than' when you leave their company? Worried about their judgement? Conscious of how negatively they made you feel about yourself? That, right there, is the epitome of a toxic friendship and as we move through this chapter, let us ask the Universe to release these connections from our lives.

WHAT QUALITIES DO YOU WANT IN A FRIEND?

Manifesting new friendships begins with creating a cosmic shopping list of qualities you'd like them to have. How do you want to feel around them? What activities would you do together? Describe the little quirks that make them unique.

Perhaps you're on a journey to feeling physically stronger and you crave someone to go hiking with at the weekend. Or maybe you are looking for a fellow single friend who wants to dance the night away with you, drinking cocktails and spilling the gossip on your latest date.

Do you want someone to laugh with? Someone who resonates with the current season you're in (for example, parenthood)? Someone who likes trying new restaurants or is building a business, just like you? Or perhaps, just as I once was, you are looking for a friend who embraces manifestation so you can share those big dreams of yours?

BE THE FRIEND YOU WANT TO ATTRACT

We know by now that the energy we put out into the world is the energy we receive back. Are you the type of friend you'd desire in your life? For example, if you are manifesting a friendship with someone who is caring, notices the small things and remembers important dates, ask yourself: are you currently doing this for the people in your life?

If you want a friendship that feels fun and spontaneous, how can you bring more of that into your life right now? If you want a friend who is clear with communication and always honest, where can you communicate better in your life right now and welcome more honesty across your relationships?

HAVE AN ENERGETIC CLEAR-OUT

If you recognize toxic friendships in your life, perhaps now is the time to re-evaluate who deserves your focus. We all go through challenging seasons in life, and I want to remind you that this is not about moving away from a friend in need. However, if you have someone in your life who constantly makes you feel bad about yourself, puts you down, drains you and doesn't treat you well, then that energy needs decluttering. You are worthy of equal, balanced, supportive, soulmate friendships. And the Universe can help deliver those when you rid yourself of energy vampires and people who make you feel 'less than'.

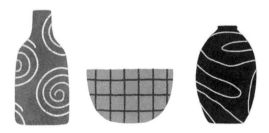

HOW CAN YOU MEET THE UNIVERSE HALFWAY?

Let's consider where your soulmate friendships might be. For example, if you are a new parent, could you discover new friendships at a sensory class or baby yoga? If you are looking for someone who is creative and likes to try new things, maybe a pottery workshop or wild swimming could be the place to get talking? Or if you're looking for a business bestie, maybe a co-working space could be worth a try?

As daunting as it may seem, I have seen many a friendship blossom from a simple share online, asking to meet people with similar interests. Meet the Universe halfway and take inspired action when you feel the nudge.

CREATE A FRIENDSHIP VISION BOARD

Creating a vision board specifically for the friendships you are calling into your life is a great way to remind yourself not only about the energy you are attracting, but also the energy you are putting out into the world.

Find images online or in magazines that resonate with the activities you imagine doing together, with the way you'll feel with a friendship that fills your cup, with words that align with your vision, and so on. Perhaps there are images of people at a retreat, or two people laughing together. A tip if you are using Pinterest as your source of images is to type in 'friendship goals', 'friendship aesthetic' or 'best friend vibes'.

Every time you look at this board, whether it be a digital board that you use as a phone screensaver or a physical board you hang up at home, sink into the energy of how grateful you are knowing those friendships are on their way to you.

HOW DO I NAVIGATE A NEGATIVE FAMILY MEMBER OR FRIEND WHEN I AM TRYING TO DEVELOP A MORE POSITIVE MINDSET?

Have you ever tried making a conscious shift to cultivating a more positive mindset, but someone in close proximity dampened your spirits? I have certainly battled with energy vampires over the years, and because of this I have developed a toolkit of tried-and-tested techniques that allow me to regain control over my own energy and emotions – because, remember, someone only has the power to make you feel a certain way if you allow them to.

MODEL OF REALITY
The first thing to acknowledge is that we all experience a different model of reality. Our model of reality refers to the way we understand the world around us. It encompasses our beliefs, knowledge, assumptions and bias, which collectively shape how we interpret the world and make sense of

information and experiences. For example, cultural norms, values and social conditioning play a significant role in shaping a person's model of reality. These influences can lead to different interpretations of the same information based on our cultural background or social context. It is worth acknowledging each person's model of reality when we are trying to understand their negative frame of mind.

WHAT MAGIC DOES THE PERSON OFFER?

It is very easy to focus on the negative parts of a person when they themselves are radiating a negative energy. However, this is only breathing life into something you do not wish to experience. Instead, how can we focus on the glimmers of magic they offer? For example, if you have a negative family member who has the ability to open the heavens as soon as the sun appears, instead of focusing on what is lacking in this relationship, can you look at what they might offer instead?

Do they give you great advice when you ask about work? Are they able to advise you on what that constant rattle is in your car? Perhaps they find joy in cooking and you're able to lift the mood by asking for their favourite recipe. Maybe you ask for their film recommendations, or you highlight just how amazing their garden looks after a season of nurturing and tending to their seeds. What glimmers can you seek?

REDIRECT CONVERSATIONS

One of the quickest ways to rebalance the energy when you notice it moving in a downward spiral is by subtly redirecting the conversation. Stop the lack mindset in its tracks by focusing on something else. This can be done in a gentle way, such as acknowledging their opinion and then changing the subject.

EVALUATE YOUR RELATIONSHIP

If someone is consistently spiralling in a pity party of negativity and you feel yourself sinking instead of swimming, it might be worth evaluating just how much time you allow yourself to spend with that person. Do you need to limit the availability they have to you? For example, if they constantly post negative things online, rather than unfriending them can you simply mute their account? Or if you struggle with their constant stream of complaining via messages, can you mute them until you are in a better place to reply.

AFFIRMATIONS FOR MOVING BACK INTO A POSITIVE STATE OF BEING

- I am in control of my thoughts and emotions.
- I choose to focus on positivity and let go of negativity.
- I am resilient, and I can handle any negativity that comes my way.
- I attract positivity and repel negativity.
- I am surrounded by love, support and positive energy.
- I release all negative energy from my mind and body.
- I am worthy of happiness and positivity.
- I choose to rise above negativity and stay in my positive zone.
- I am responsible for my own happiness, and I choose positivity.
- I am a beacon of light and negativity cannot extinguish my shine.
- I focus on solutions, not problems.

Q

HOW CAN I MANIFEST MORE LOVE WITHIN MY FAMILY?

Manifesting more love within your family begins with your current thoughts and language. What narrative and stories are you repeating on a daily basis? That no one appreciates you? That no one listens to you? That there is always an argument to be had? Are these stories centred around feelings of unappreciation, lack of communication or constant arguments? It's essential to recognize the narratives you've created and their impact on your family relationships. Negative thought patterns can manifest as self-fulfilling prophecies, reinforcing the very issues you wish to change.

If our thoughts create our reality, what thoughts are you digesting right now? If you constantly dwell on negative aspects of your family life, you may inadvertently attract more of the same. Instead, try to shift your focus towards positive aspects of your family, acknowledging moments of love and connection, no matter how small they may seem.

Another thing to consider is how can you lead by example? How can you be the source of love within your family unit? For example,

how can you show appreciation, express your feelings and practise active listening? When you demonstrate love and kindness, it's more likely to be reciprocated by others in your household.

Which leads on perfectly to the art of giving without being attached to the outcome. When you give love and affection to your family, do so without attaching expectations or conditions to your actions. Unconditional love is a powerful force that can transform relationships. But if you offer love with the sole intent of receiving something in return, it might not create the genuine connection you desire. Instead, give freely from your heart, expecting nothing in return but the joy of giving.

Where in your daily life can you provide opportunities for more love? This is what we call putting the action into the Law of Attraction and offering the Universe different routes to be able to amplify more love in your family. Practical steps include spending quality time together, fostering connection and creating traditions. It's also key to encourage open communication within your family and create a safe space for everyone to share thoughts and feelings. Small acts of kindness, such as helping one another with chores, leaving little notes around the house, or even just a hug can magnetize more love into the family.

Finally, be patient. When it comes to anything within the realm of manifestation, gripping tightly will only strangle your desire. Changes might not occur overnight but patience allows for growth, understanding and gradual improvements. Slow and steady wins the race, remember.

SMALL ACTS OF KINDNESS AT HOME

- Surprise your family with a favourite homemade meal.
- Take a moment to express gratitude for something specific that a family member has done for you.
- Leave little notes with words of affection or encouragement in unexpected places for your family to find.
- Sometimes, a simple hug will do more than words ever could.
- Pay close attention when a family member is speaking and show that you value their thoughts and feelings.
- Give sincere compliments to family members.
- Organize fun activities or game nights to create closer connections.
- Compile a playlist of songs that each family member loves and play it during family gatherings.
- Recognize and celebrate each family member's achievements, no matter how small.
- Surprise a family member with breakfast in bed on a special occasion or just 'because'.
- Don't forget to say 'I love you' regularly, and mean it. These three words hold immense power.

ARE THERE MANIFESTATION TECHNIQUES I COULD DO WITH A FRIEND?

Having a supportive, like-minded friend who embraces manifestation just as much as you can feel like a gift from the Universe in itself. There are a number of techniques and activities that you can do with a friend/group of friends to amplify your energy. In this instance, there truly is magic in numbers.

FULL MOON PARTY

Approximately every 28 days, the moon appears fully illuminated from Earth's perspective. This is what we call the full moon. Spiritually, it is said to be a powerful time to release what is no longer serving us. The completion of a cycle, if you like. The perfect time to let go of limiting beliefs and stories before we set intentions under the next phase of the moon.

During your Full Moon Party, invite friends around, creating somewhere comfortable to sit and providing everyone with a piece of paper and pen. As you listen to soothing music, take some time to write down what each of you would like to release under the full moon, then go around the circle and share at least one thing from your list. Maybe it is self-sabotage, or constantly allowing your inner critic to drown out the voice of compassion. Maybe it's allowing people to overstep your boundaries, or snoozing through your alarm and then rushing in the morning.

Tear each piece of paper into strips and add either to a fire indoors, or a fire outside that you can responsibly manage. As the papers burn and the smoke rises, notice how the energy lifts in the group. You could even ask each person to recite the phrase 'I thank you for keeping me safe but now I choose to release you' as they add their paper to the flames.

MAGNETIC VOICE NOTES

Speaking about your manifestations as if they have already come to fruition is a powerful way to become a magnetic force – and what better way to do that than with your best friend? When you have decided to manifest something into your life, record a voice note for your friend, talking as if this is already your reality. Describe in detail how you feel, how your life has changed for the better. Include what you see, what you hear, and what you can envision next. When your friend returns with their own magnetizing voice note, be sure to listen with excited enthusiasm. Go back and forth, asking questions and sharing how passionate you are about each other's dream life.

FUTURE YOU WEEKEND

This is a weekend where you live how you envision your future self to live. Except during this exercise, you are intensifying the magic by inviting your friends along for the fun. For example, how does Future You spend your Sunday? During a Future You Weekend, create just that. What morning routine does Future You have? Even if you dream of running along the beach and you live 300 miles inland, can you and your friend find yourselves a nice local route for that morning run regardless?

Perhaps you imagine having a hot date lined up for a Saturday evening. Can you and your bestie book somewhere special to eat together to lean into that energy – and perhaps catch the eye of a potential future hot date!? Does Future You shop until they drop? Could you embrace that energy of abundance and go into your favourite shops to try outfits on together? Perhaps Future You spends their weekend out in nature, wild swimming, finding hidden waterfalls. Grab your friend and make that your current reality!

HOW CAN I INTRODUCE THE CONCEPT OF MANIFESTATION TO CHILDREN?

Whether you are a parent, aunt, uncle, guardian or even mentor, introducing the magic of manifestation to children can help encourage them to believe in their dreams, set goals, and work towards achieving them. It also helps build a positive mindset and increased focus on gratitude, nurturing their creativity and self-belief.

SIMPLIFY THE CONCEPT
To introduce manifestation to children, start by simplifying the concept. Manifestation, in essence, means believing in the power of your thoughts and intentions to create your reality. Break this down into simpler terms, explaining that when they truly believe in something and work towards it, then it's more likely to happen. Use relatable examples like wanting to learn a new skill, making a new friend or achieving a specific grade in school.

STORYTELLING AND VISUALIZATION

Children often respond well to storytelling and visualization. Share stories or read books that feature characters who achieve their dreams through determination and positive thinking. Encourage your child to close their eyes and imagine themselves in the shoes of these characters, experiencing the journey towards their goals.

ENCOURAGE POSITIVE AFFIRMATIONS

Teach children the power of positive affirmations. Create a list of affirmations with them, such as 'I am clever', 'I am kind' or 'I can achieve anything I set my mind to'. Encourage them to repeat these affirmations daily. You could even recite them together on the journey to school or while you're making breakfast. This habit is incredibly effective when instilled at a young age.

GOAL SETTING

Help children set achievable goals. Start with small, age-appropriate objectives like completing a puzzle, learning a new word or scoring well on a quiz. Break bigger goals into smaller steps, making them less intimidating. Regularly check in with their progress and celebrate the mini milestones they achieve along the way.

VISION BOARDS

Creating a vision board is an engaging way to introduce manifestation to children. Provide magazines, scissors, glue and a posterboard, and encourage them to cut out images or words that represent their dreams. They can then paste these on the board, creating a visual reminder of what they want to manifest in their lives – plus, what better way to spend a high-vibe afternoon together than getting crafty.

POSITIVE ROLE MODELS

Introduce children to positive role models who have achieved their dreams through belief, taking aligned action and determination. Share stories of famous athletes, scientists, artists or even family members who have overcome challenges in their lives. This demonstrates that manifestation is not an abstract concept, but actually a practical approach to life.

TEACH RESILIENCE

Something to be reminded of is that no matter what age you are, manifestation doesn't mean everything will appear like magic. Emphasize the importance of resilience and perseverance to the children in your life. Explain that setbacks are a natural part of the journey and can be valuable learning experiences. Encourage them to adapt and keep working towards their dreams.

PRACTISE GRATITUDE

Teaching children the value of gratitude is incredibly powerful. Encourage them to keep a gratitude journal where they write down things they are thankful for each day. This helps shift their focus towards positivity and attracts more of what they appreciate into their lives.

KEEP IT FUN

Make learning about manifestation an enjoyable experience. Engage in activities like guided meditation, creative arts and crafts, or even playful visualization exercises. The more enjoyable you make manifestation, the more likely it is that children will embrace the concept. And before you know it, they're manifesting a trip to Disneyland and taking aligned action by finding your passport.

IS IT POSSIBLE TO MANIFEST FOR SOMEONE ELSE IN YOUR LIFE?

There is a wealth of conflicting advice in response to this question from spiritual gurus and manifestation guides. Some believe it's not possible to manifest for another person, while some agree it is. I am in the latter camp. This is because I myself have successfully manifested for others in my life. I have also received a plethora of stories sharing similar circumstances.

Do I think you can manifest for someone else and forcibly change their life path towards something unaligned? No. I think that is what we call spiritual manipulation. This is something I touched upon when answering the question, 'How do I manifest my ex back?' (see page 47). The key thing to remember when manifesting for someone else is that your desire for the end goal should be in total alignment. You both have to want the same thing. You both need to desire the same harmonious outcome.

When both parties involved genuinely share the same vision and believe it to be for the greater good, doubling down on positive energy can only ever be a good thing. An advantage of manifesting for someone else is that you may encounter less resistance compared to when you're manifesting for yourself. The inner critic, which often casts doubts and scepticism, tends to be quieter in such scenarios, making the manifestation journey smoother. Visualization is key to manifesting for someone else – not just imagining scenarios of the outcome for the other person, but for yourself too. Visualize the phone call you'll get to share the good news or the conversation you'll have, perhaps as you celebrate.

A MANIFESTING SUCCESS STORY

I have received many stories of manifesting for someone else over the years, and I would like to share a particularly powerful story from one of my clients, Kimberly Duran:

'I manifested my husband being made redundant, as odd as that may seem. He had been working at the same company for 20 years, but we both knew how unhappy he was. I began manifesting him a much better job, and visualized him coming home to tell me the good news. Within a week of my manifesting on a daily basis, he was given his redundancy notice. The next day he sent his CV to a company he really wanted to work for, and despite them not having any current openings, I still visualized them offering him a job. Within 20 minutes, he had a call from the managing director of the branch asking if he could come in for an interview the next day. When he arrived, they had the new starter paperwork all filled out, offering him the position. He came home to tell me he got the job, exactly as I had visualized!'

CAN I MANIFEST A PEACEFUL RESOLUTION TO A FALLING-OUT?

Conflict is a natural part of human existence. There will be times when our views don't match other people's, and in the heat of the moment, navigating our vast range of emotions, we say things we regret or act out of character. However, it is possible for you to bring forth a peaceful resolution using manifestation, if both parties desire this at their core. The key is to bring your energy into harmony with how you will feel when a resolution has been met. Will you feel relieved? Happy? Like you've taken a big sigh and your shoulders have dropped?

LETTER OF RESOLUTION

Letter of Resolution is a manifestation technique I created that asks you to write a letter to the person you are in conflict with. The letter doesn't need to be physically sent, of course, as the object of this exercise is to help you access the feelings of peace and relief that come with understanding both points of view in a dispute. Here's how to write your Letter of Resolution:

Step 1 Before you begin writing your letter, put yourself in the shoes of the person you are in conflict with. Why might they have certain views? What could be causing them to feel a particular way? Understanding and empathy are easier to access once you've given space to the situation.

Step 2 Explain your side of the conflict and why you may have reacted in the way you did. Understanding how both parties hold some form of responsibility can help you reach a peaceful outcome faster.

Step 3 Write down all the reasons you are grateful for your friendship/relationship and the positive effects it has had on your life. Remind yourself of the magic that once magnetized you to them. Lean into that energy as much as you can.

Step 4 Finish your letter with forgiveness, both for the other person and yourself.

Step 5 Visualize the other person reading this letter and imagine how their energy begins to align to yours, attracting each other towards a positive reconciliation.

Step 6 Put your Letter of Resolution under your pillow, asking the Universe to send healing energy to the other party and for a peaceful resolution to manifest.

RECEIVING RESOLUTION

Now release your need for an apology. When you 'need' something, you are saying to the Universe that you lack it. That you don't believe it is yours. And when we are in the energy of lack, we attract more reasons to feel lack into our lives. The apology, if desired, has already happened energetically before it appears in the physical realm, so release your grip on this desired outcome.

The most important thing to remember is: be open to different forms of communication and potential solutions. Continue to visualize the resolution you desire as if it were already a reality. The Universe could deliver resolution in both expected and unexpected ways.

A PERSONAL EXAMPLE

At the age of ten I fell out with my best friend. While at the time I didn't understand that what I was doing was called manifestation, I spent some time daydreaming about being friends again. Within the hour, she called my house phone. Except she hadn't meant to. She had accidentally dialled my house number, and whether coincidentally or magically with a little help from the Universe, we were forced to talk and were reunited as the Ultimate BFFs (best friends forever).

While the plan here isn't to wait by the phone and make up as quickly as ten year olds, this example shows how the Universe could deliver resolution in a way you haven't imagined just yet. Be patient and in the meantime, focus on gratitude and other elements of joy in your life.

HOME

HOW DO I MANIFEST MY DREAM HOME?

Whether you are renting your first apartment or want to move up the property ladder to your forever family home, taking aligned action can help you move forward in this new chapter of your life with ease and flow.

DREAM HOUSE VISION BOARD

What do you want your dream home to have? A large garden? A rooftop deck? A pantry? A reading nook? Create your cosmic shopping list and then get to work on creating a Dream House Vision Board, either a traditional cut-and-stick version, or by finding inspiration on Pinterest to craft a digital board. Visualize yourself there. Create a film in your mind showing you getting the keys on that first day and opening the door to your new home. Imagine walking into the kitchen and opening your cupboards to be greeted by everything organized and neatly labelled. See yourself watering the flowers in your garden or tending to the herbs you've planted. Fluffing up your cushions on your white cloud sofa or running a bubble bath in your clawfoot tub. Imagine yourself really living in the space.

LIVE LIKE A LOCAL

The next stop is to live like a local, taking time to explore different neighbourhoods and acting as if you've already moved in. You could take a walk around the streets of where you wish to live. Say hello to your future neighbours. Grab a coffee in what could be your new favourite spot. Book a class at the local gym. Throughout this book, I talk about how important 'acting as if' is to the manifestation process. Like attracts like, remember. So, when we're in the energy of already living in our dream neighbourhood, acting as if we've already moved in, the Universe can get to work delivering opportunities to help us energetically match just that.

TAKE ALIGNED ACTION

Aligned action could see you contacting local agents and letting them know the criteria of your dream house, what budget you have available and what neighbourhoods you're looking at. Set up alerts to be notified as soon as something comes up for rent or goes on the market for sale.

GET READY TO MOVE

The Law of Assumption, a universal law alongside the Law of Attraction, is the concept of assuming that what we desire is already ours. What we believe to be true becomes our reality. So with that said, what better way to

assume that our dream house is on its way to us than to start decluttering and packing up our current living situation, ready to move when the time is right. While living out of cardboard boxes for the foreseeable future isn't necessarily the vibe you want, you could begin going through your cupboards, drawers, and so on, and deciding what you will be taking into this next chapter with you. Out with old, stagnant energy and in with the new.

APPRECIATE YOUR CURRENT HOME

Great things appear when we're grateful for what we already have, so embrace all of the things you can feel thankful for in your current living environment. It may not be perfect, but what elements do you appreciate? Make a list and remind yourself of this often. Perhaps it's hot running water? The natural light? Space in your wardrobe? Somewhere comfortable to sit? Focusing on what you have, rather than what you lack, will shift your energy almost instantly.

LOOK FOR SIGNS

Now, this is where divine timing comes into play. We know from the introduction of this book that the 'how' and 'when' are not ours to control when it comes to co-creating with the Universe. We share our desire, we take aligned action, we release, and only then do we receive when the time is right. However, that doesn't mean you can't keep your eyes and ears open for signs that might lead you to discovering your dream home.

Maybe a friend will mention a house that has become available in the area you're interested in, or you'll suddenly see an email from a local agent. Perhaps you'll overhear a conversation when you're living like a local about a new development that sparks your interest. Or maybe you'll spot a 'For Sale' sign as you feel drawn to take a detour through the area. Trust any nudges that come through and follow them.

BE OPEN-MINDED

Finally, go into this chapter of your life with an open mind – while a house may not look perfect on the outside, don't judge a book by its cover. Trust in the directions you are being called in, whether they're designed to reaffirm what you definitely don't want or to open your eyes to the potential of something you've not thought about before. The Universe might just be leading you to magic.

AFFIRMATIONS FOR MANIFESTING YOUR DREAM HOME

- My dream home brings me so much joy and comfort, and I am ready to build my future there.
- My dream home is already mine and I trust the Universe to deliver it in perfect timing.
- I am so grateful that my dream home is available for me to move in and make it my own.
- The excited and joyful energy I radiate is magnetizing my dream home to me.
- My dream home is manifesting easily and effortlessly, and I am ready to embrace this next chapter of my life.

THE HOUSE I LOVED FELL THROUGH AT THE LAST MINUTE. DID I MANIFEST THIS?

The short answer is yes. But before you slam this book shut and toss it in the bin, let me explain. Not everything we think we want manifests into reality. I have witnessed this time and time again over the years: people attracting what they think is their dream house, only for it to then subsequently fall through at the last moment. There is no denying the disappointment we feel when something we desire fails to materialize, whether that be a dream house, a dream job or a dream date, for example.

SURRENDER TO THE UNIVERSE
However, what if I told you that it was always meant to be this way? That every time I have been privy to someone losing their dream house, a few months later I've witnessed them finding something even more suitable? What if I told you how many times I've heard the words, 'We thought that was our dream house but in hindsight we can see why it wasn't'?

There will always be a reason why your dream house didn't materialize. Often it is future stresses that we can't see in

the present, but the Universe is aware of. It might seem like your dream house on paper, but in reality, there could be a plethora of reasons why it's not suitable under the surface (sometimes quite literally in the foundations of the home). Perhaps the neighbours are night owls and you're an early bird who likes a quiet environment after 10pm. Or maybe the commute is much longer than you imagine when you take into consideration rush hour traffic. Maybe there are so many problems in the house masked with a plaster to secure the sale that you'd have to gut each room and pour all of your savings into it. Maybe your landlord ignores all requests once you've signed the agreement and you've paid the deposit.

With anything in life, you will be guided down the path of least resistance. It may feel confusing at times because the path of least resistance doesn't automatically mean there won't be emotional challenges, especially when we're wrestling with our need to control the outcome. But this is where learning to trust and have faith in the long game really comes into play. When we release our grip on what we think should happen and are open to the possibility of what *could* happen instead, that's where the Universe really gets to shine.

A useful affirmation for this is: 'It's either this, or something better.' This means the Universe will help co-create what you've asked for or present you with something even better than you could have ever imagined. Something better suited to you. Something that caters for dreams you didn't even realize you needed fulfilling. Just hold the faith and in hindsight you'll see.

REFRAME DISAPPOINTMENT

It is hard to see the silver lining of a cloud when all around you feels foggy with disappointment and shattered dreams. But a great way to reframe this is to make a list of all the reasons why your manifestation not materializing is, in fact, a positive thing. When we focus on the negative, it exacerbates that feeling even more. Switch your focus to why this might be a positive change in direction. For example, maybe this change presents more time to save. Perhaps the move would have coincided with an already busy season in your life. Maybe now you can refine your list of specifics, adding more of what you'd like from your future dream home. Perhaps you were blindsided originally by the view of what you thought was your dream home and compromised on the amount of space.

CAN I MANIFEST MORE PEACE IN MY CURRENT LIVING SITUATION?

Whether you are struggling to live with your parents or roommates who are less than desirable, or you're in the midst of a broken-down relationship, it can be incredibly challenging to remain high-vibe when your living situation feels chaotic. The good news is that it is possible to manifest more peace within your home. And it all starts with you.

WHAT ENERGY ARE YOU EMITTING?

The first thing to check is what energy you are emitting in the house. Often, when we find ourselves in tense situations, our natural response is to match with a similar energy. However, that can magnetize more of the same, which is a negative cycle to be stuck in. You have the power to shift your state of being from the second you wake up. How might life feel if you choose a more empathetic, understanding approach? I get it. Sometimes it's hard to be empathetic to an inconsiderate roommate who uses all the hot water and forgets to close the fridge door. But you have the choice to either let that ruin the rest of your day or release it and continue manifesting a better living situation (and perhaps roommate). You may even start to notice that when you shift your energy to a more positive frequency, it is mirrored by the people you live with.

HOW DO YOU COMMUNICATE?

Calm, clear communication is necessary for a happy living situation. Understand what boundaries need to be set and lay those out – again, in a calm way. Entering a situation with demands is likely to be met with resistance. Use your journal beforehand to write down the points you'd like to communicate. What is the resolution you desire? Imagine that has come to fruition – how do you feel? What can you see around you? What can you hear? Create a mind movie that plays out exactly how you want the scenario to go and understand how you can embody that version of you now. Do you feel calmer? More at peace? Relieved? Embrace that energy before you communicate and notice if there is a shift in the energy you receive back.

HOW CAN YOU RECONNECT?

Sometimes the key to a happier household is reconnecting to the people you share your space with and remembering their humanity. Let's take your parents, for example. How can you connect with them in a way that feels organic? Can you ask them more questions and truly listen to the answers?

Can you try your hand at a hobby of theirs and ask for their help? Rather than leaning into people-pleasing tendencies, we are aiming to increase the frequency of the household with reconnection and understanding. If you have a roommate who you're struggling to live with, for example, can you embrace their humanity and chat over drinks in front of a good film?

WHAT DO YOU BELIEVE TO BE REALITY?

What you believe will create your experience. It really is that simple. We have access to an endless possibility of thoughts at any given time and the subconscious mind accepts each thought as a command. Regardless of whether that thought is negative or positive, the subconscious will go in search of proof that it is true. This is called your confirmation bias. For example, if you believe your roommate is always loud, or you expect your parents to continuously question your whereabouts, every door closing or 'where are you going?' will only reaffirm your frustrations – even though it may originate from a place of innocence. We experience what we believe to be true. What do you want your experience to be instead? Change your focus to this reality and notice what the subconscious begins to spot.

CAN I MANIFEST A HOLIDAY?

Whether you're craving cocktails on the beach as the sun sets or hiking in the forest before toasting marshmallows under the stars, manifesting a break away from everyday life is absolutely possible. There are a number of ways you can connect to the Universe to do this, starting with getting clear on your vision of what a dream break away would look like.

TRAVEL BOARD
Begin by pulling together images that represent the kind of holiday you want to manifest. It could be pictures of the Amalfi Coast or taking a campervan on a road trip. It could be images of campfires or a quiet lakeside lodge, surrounded by trees. Get specific about the experience you are calling in. Do you want a holiday full of adventure, or relaxation? What destination do you want to visit? What activities do you want to do? Once you've created your vision board, make a habit of checking in regularly to remind yourself of the excitement you'll feel when that holiday manifests into reality.

VISUALIZE YOURSELF ON HOLIDAY

Create a vivid film in your mind of you on holiday, enjoying the sights, sounds and scents around you. What do you see? What do you hear? What do you smell? What can you taste? What do you feel? Ignite your senses and allow yourself to sink into that potent energy of being on holiday, switching off from the real world for a moment.

TAKE INSPIRED ACTION

How can you take aligned action towards your goal of manifesting a holiday? Research the destination. Look at flight prices and times. Plan trips and excursions. Save images on Instagram of popular hotspots to come back to. Create a capsule wardrobe. Dig out your passport. Enter competitions. Tell other people about your plans. Check your holiday allowance. Dust off your suitcase. Look at different ways you could manifest money into your life – perhaps by starting a passion project, selling things you no longer need or use, applying for refunds, and so on.

EXPECT THE UNEXPECTED

The most important thing to remember is that manifesting a holiday can come in many different forms. I can recall stories of people winning holidays, being gifted a break away by their parents, being invited to an all-expenses-paid wedding, being gifted enough money to cover their dream destination, receiving a large refund that enabled them to book a trip away, and travelling with their partner on a work trip to their vision-board location. When we release the 'how' and 'when', the Universe can begin to co-create our dreams in the most unexpected ways.

WAYS TO EMBODY YOUR HOLIDAY AT HOME

- Light a candle with a scent linked to your dream destination, such as coconut or cedarwood.

- Put on sunscreen every morning, as you do when preparing for a day in the sun.

- Buy a new holiday-inspired book and carve out time to read it each day.

- Experiment with different recipes, including the ingredients local to your dream destination.

- Get up earlier and enjoy the sunrise or watch the sunset over a homemade cocktail.

- Embrace a slower pace of life, taking things off your to-do list and being more intentional with your day.

- Drink more water and stay hydrated.

- Wear your favourite holiday outfits at home.

- Embrace your local town or city as a tourist and create a bucket list of new places to discover.

- Be more adventurous every day and say yes to more opportunities.

WHAT ARE SOME WAYS IN WHICH I CAN INCORPORATE FENG SHUI INTO MY HOME TO ENHANCE MY MANIFESTATION PRACTICES?

Your home is an energetic extension of who you are, so creating a sacred space is essential to feeling aligned and empowered in your manifesting abilities. For this answer, let us turn to the ancient Chinese practice of feng shui to help create more balance and invite positive chi into your home.

DECLUTTER REGULARLY

Clutter can block the flow of energy within your home, especially if you're holding on to things that have a negative attachment, such as gifts from past partners. Visit each room and donate, sell or throw away anything that no longer feels aligned to your highest self. Even removing clothes that no longer make you feel great about yourself and filling your wardrobe with pieces that you love can produce an incredible shift in your baseline frequency.

RELEASE OLD ENERGY

It is important to open all doors and windows on a regular basis to clear old energy and welcome in a flow of new energy. Allow natural light to fill your home, bringing with it a wealth of positive energy. Schedule a regular ritual, lighting incense, palo santo or a bundle of herbs (like sage or lavender) to smoke cleanse each room. As you do this, ask any negative energy to leave through the open windows and doors, and set your intentions for fresh, positive energy to expand.

NAVIGATE THE FLOW

It is important that there is a natural flow of energy within the home. Avoid furniture placements that block exits or restrict movement, and arrange the furniture in each room to allow for a natural, open flow of energy.

BUILD YOUR WEALTH CORNER

Using the Bagua Map, a feng shui energy map, identify the different areas of your home and their corresponding life themes. Wealth and prosperity, for example, is located in the back left corner of the home when you stand in front of the formal entrance. To enhance this part of your life, keep this area clean and well lit. Add crystals like citrine, tiger's eye and pyrite (known for their wealth qualities), a bowl of coins, and a plant such as a jade plant. Use decor with curved lines, water and wood and embrace the colours purple, gold and red.

UTILIZE THE POWER OF MIRRORS

Mirrors in feng shui are believed to reflect and amplify energy, so place them strategically to expand the energy of abundance and manifestation – position a mirror to reflect a beautiful view, your vision board, or symbols of your goals, or place one on your desk if your back is facing the door. Within feng shui it is said that facing away from the door is like turning your back on opportunities that might arise, so a mirror on your desk will reflect said opportunities right back to you.

EMBRACE MORE PLANTS
Not only do indoor plants reduce stress and boost our mood, they also bring positive energy into our home. The bamboo plant is renowned within feng shui for increasing the vibration of a house, specifically around attracting wealth. Other plants you may want to consider buying for yourself, or for others as a housewarming present, include a jade plant (or the money plant as it is often called), a money tree, which is seen as a symbol for good luck, and lavender for its healing properties.

HOW DO I CARVE SPACE IN A BUSY HOUSEHOLD FOR MY SPIRITUAL SELF-CARE?

With children, pets, family, jobs, relationships, running a household and living life, it's no wonder the question 'but when?!' comes up repeatedly when discussing spiritual self-care. Spiritual self-care is looking after your inner being. Self-care is often put to the bottom of the to-do list, an activity seen as frivolous when you're juggling the many different components of life. However, nourishing and connecting to our spiritual well-being (as well as our emotional, mental and physical health) is one of the most important things we can do.

CREATING A SACRED SPACE

Where in the house can you create a sacred space for your spiritual self-care? If space is limited, fear not. All you really need is a nook or corner somewhere away from the hustle and bustle of the household. The aim is to design a space that feels safe and comfortable, somewhere you can retreat each morning or evening and dip into your tool belt of techniques, whether that be meditating, mirror work, visualization, crystal work, tarot reading or journalling, to name just a few. The most suitable place to create your manifesting nook is your bedroom or office – somewhere out of sight from the regular footfall of the house.

TIME, BOUNDARIES AND HABITS

The most important thing to consider when you are looking to increase your spiritual self-care is when you can carve out more time for yourself. For some people, a morning routine is a no-go. And that is more than okay. Maybe 20 minutes once a week is all life allows at the moment. A hungry toddler, for example, doesn't care if you haven't meditated yet. But scheduling in that 20 minutes per week has to become non-negotiable. Create a boundary around that time for your spiritual self-care. Add it to your calendar and honour your own self-care, recognizing that when you feel in alignment, it has a ripple effect throughout the entire house.

MANIFESTING NOOK ESSENTIALS

- A floor cushion or beanbag
- Candles
- Plants
- Vision board
- Crystals
- Sound bowl
- Deck of oracle or tarot cards
- Notebook and pen
- Palo santo, incense or cleansing herbs
- Essential oils

Perhaps Sunday evenings are your time to reconnect with your highest self. When the rest of the house has gone to bed, grab your journal, play some relaxing music and make yourself comfortable in your spiritual self-care nook.

If you find yourself struggling to carve out time in this busy season of your life, then habit stacking and multitasking is where you could experience success. See page 26 to discover more manifesting techniques that you can integrate with your daily tasks.

IDEAS FOR YOUR SUNDAY SPIRITUAL RESET ROUTINE

- Pull a card from your oracle/tarot deck and journal on what comes up for you.

- Use palo santo or similar to smudge around your body and cleanse yourself of any stagnant energy holding on from the previous week.

- Meditate and feel yourself release anything that you do not want to carry into a new week.

- Reconnect to your vision board, visualizing your future self and leaning into the energy of how it feels knowing that everything you desire is already yours.

- Write a diary entry in your journal as if your ideal week has already happened: what did you experience, how did you feel, what came to fruition for you?

- Ask yourself what inspired action you can take this coming week to help you move closer to your dream life.

Q

CAN I MANIFEST PARTICULAR OBJECTS, SUCH AS A CAR?

For this answer, I want to take you back to 2016. At the time I was driving a £300 car my dad had helped me buy, a bold shade of red with turquoise wing mirrors bought as replacements from the scrapyard after a pillar in an underground car park accidentally broke off the original ones. It was far from the dream car I had on my vision board. On my vision board sat a white SUV complete with original wing mirrors, leather interior and electric windows that didn't need the glass popping back in each time they went up.

However, despite its many flaws, I knew that showing gratitude for my current red and turquoise reality, while waiting for my dream car to arrive, would be key to speeding up the manifestation process. I thanked my car for every safe journey. I spoke words of gratitude to it as we drove, even when the glass in the window continued to pop out as I manually wound it up. I treated that car as if it were brand-new. Regular trips to the car wash, a new car scent added inside. Every compartment neatly organized. There wasn't a speck of dirt to be found.

One of the biggest shifts to my energy was using visualization as I was driving and changing my physiology. Because my dream car was higher up from the road than my then-reality, I visibly moved my body to sit taller as I was driving. I would visualize my car having a white exterior as I drove along the road. I played songs that made me feel abundant and in a high vibration with each journey I took. And because I had added a new car scent, I was igniting my senses to believe that I was driving my vision-board car.

What inspired action did I take towards this manifestation to let the Universe know I was serious? I took my dream car for a test drive. At that point in time, it was out of my budget, but that didn't stop me from sitting inside, feeling how the seats moulded around my body, how the steering wheel felt, how smoothly it drove out on the road. The test drive allowed my subconscious mind to program what it felt like to drive my dream car, so it no longer felt like a wish – it was a reality.

How did my dream car manifest? A year later, I received a lump sum of money that enabled me to put a large deposit down and there it stood proudly on my driveway, my manifestation finally coming to fruition. It didn't happen overnight. It took 12 months of gratitude, visualization and belief. But I didn't waver when it came to holding the faith and trusting that the car would be mine somewhere down the line. The 'how' and 'when' weren't mine to control, but the mindset around what I wanted to manifest was. The lump sum of money I received came randomly and it was the exact amount I needed for a deposit on my vision-board car. Did I expect my manifestation to come that way? No. But that is the beauty of co-creating with the Universe. We get to experience things far beyond what we can imagine.

JOURNAL PROMPTS

- What inspired action can you take towards an object you are manifesting?

- How can you show gratitude for what you have now?

- How can you embody the version of you that already has what you desire?

- What will it feel like when your manifestation appears?

- What will you experience? What will you see, hear, smell or even taste?

FINAL THOUGHTS

As I sat at my desk, late September sun streaming in through the window, I realized as I tried in vain to draw this book to a close that it deserved more than a conclusion. Our personal growth is never-ending. The possibilities around us are never-ending. The power that manifestation has to change our lives is never-ending.

Which is why this book, despite ending in a physical sense on its final page, will continue to help guide you throughout your life. No matter what season you find yourself in, whether that be moving up the career ladder, reconnecting with spiritual self-care, or attracting more abundance into your bank account, I hope that you feel drawn back time and time again.

I have witnessed just how powerful the act of conscious manifesting can be. Not only in my own life, but in the lives of the thousands of people I have taught across the world. These aren't stories of manifesting millions, fast cars and mansions. But rather stories of manifesting a much-needed text message from an estranged parent. Stories of welcoming a lump sum of money that felt life-changing in that moment. Tales of winning family trips away, or job promotions that meant someone could finally pay for a garden renovation.

Small but mighty manifestations that increase the overall happiness of our everyday lives. Because at the heart of everything I teach, including the words I have crafted in this book, lies happiness. Connecting with the Universe, tuning into gratitude, understanding what we desire in our soul away from the 'shoulds' of society and social media – it all comes down to creating a life we truly love.
I hope this book helps you do just that.

ACKNOWLEDGEMENTS

When the opportunity came around to write a second book, I hesitated. Not because I didn't have the words, but because I wasn't sure I could navigate the challenging year I was having health-wise, alongside pouring my heart into this book. I needn't have worried. The support I received from friends, family, the team at Octopus Publishing – Louisa, Nicky, Agnes, Alex, Caroline, Juliette, Ros, Hazel, Rosa, Lucy and Nic – and the Universe itself has been nothing short of magic. And as I started to feel healthier and become stronger, I found writing this book to be almost therapeutic. Downloading my brain onto the pages, if you like. My biggest thank you, however, goes to the beautiful souls inside my community. The people who share their manifestations with me. Those who ask questions, and share their fears as well as their wins. The ones who take action. Who embrace my teachings in their everyday lives. Who write heartfelt letters and trust me with their biggest secrets as if we've known each other for years. Thank you. Thank you for supporting my vision. My dreams for The Manifestation Collective. And for everything I am manifesting into my life. This book is for you.